MR SINGH'S FABULOUS FIERY COOKBOOK

MR
SINGH'S
FABULOUS FIERY
COOKBOOK

ANGLO-ASIAN FUSION RECIPES WITH BITE

PAVILION

CONTENTS

WELCOME

Firstly, on behalf of my family and I, thank you so much for choosing to buy our book and for sharing our love of coming together through food.

We are Mr. Singh's and there are 7 of us: Hardev (Poppa Singh, AKA Pops), Kamal (mum) and us, the children. My brother Rav (with the tattoos), his wife Sonia (with the big smile), their gorgeous son Neev, Sukhi (the handsome young gun), my wife Amar (with the pretty eyes) and finally me, Kuldip Singh Sahota (tall, dark and handsome – joking!). I will be your guide throughout this book and will introduce you to everyone.

A few years ago, we started making Mr. Singh's Hot Punjabi Chilli Sauce in our garden shed and over time we have been fortunate enough for the business to grow so that our sauce is now available in supermarkets nationwide, we export our products internationally, and have appeared all over the press and been featured on TV. The last few years have been a blur of activity and it still feels like our journey has only just begun.

Both of my parents have four brothers and a sister each. Yes, each! And each of their siblings had two to three children each. This means that my brothers and I were fortunate enough to grow up with over 24 riotous first cousins, three sets of grandparents and 18 uncles and aunts.

When you start totting up the numbers, you can imagine how much work went into the family 'popping over for lunch' in our family's small East London terrace. Food has always played a large part in shaping our family. Recipes are passed down through the generations and we have always come together to celebrate and share good times over food (and a drink or two!).

This abundance of love, personality, energy and creativity gave us the opportunity to grow up enjoying the amazing food of our heritage, as well as spicy twists on

Mr Singh's Fabulous Fiery Cookbook

Rav and I muching our way through Mum's homemade lunch on a long family roadtrip through Kenya.

traditional British food – multiple bags of fish and chips were given a Punjabi twist because Grandma found the chips bland, and Popa Singh's Kenyan Kebabs were slathered in tomato ketchup and enjoyed between two slices of stodgy bread by us children.

Today, "us kids" (as we describe ourselves) have grown up and are either married or in relationships and are starting to have children of our own. As our family grows, so does our love of enjoying food together. At any opportunity we will come together to eat, drink and be merry.

Contained in this book, you will find a selection of recipes we were raised with and feel privileged to share. You will find seven distinct personalities in our family and its food, which is reflected in the range of dishes for you to enjoy.

No helmet?! Pops throws caution to the wind astride a scooter in India.

Some of them are simple with European origins (what my generation has grown up with), others may have Kenyan influences (where my parents and grandparents were born) and finally there are more traditional Punjabi (North West India) dishes as this is where our ancestors are from.

Ultimately, my family and I would love for you to bring together your friends, family and loved ones to enjoy the food which gives us so much joy.

If you are ever in East London, please do call by and come over for a cup of Punjabi Tea (page 36), you will always be welcome. Thank you once again for choosing this book and I really hope it gives you as much joy to read as it has given us to write.

With kindest regards,
Kuldip Singh Sahota

Some very dapper gents enjoying a beer at a family gathering in the 1970s. Second from left is Mum's brother, third from left and first from right are both Pop's brothers.

🔥🔥🔥🔥🔥🔥🔥🔥🔥🔥🔥🔥🔥🔥🔥🔥🔥🔥🔥🔥🔥🔥🔥
A BRIEF HISTORY OF CHILLI

Chilli peppers have been a part of the human diet for more than 6,000 years, originating in and around what is modern-day Mexico.

History tells us that a Diego Alvarez Chanca, a physician aboard Christopher Columbus' second voyage to the West Indies in 1493, brought the first chilli peppers to Spain and first wrote about their medicinal effects in 1494. From here, the spread of chilli peppers to Asia was most likely via its introduction to Portuguese traders who promoted its commerce in the Asian spice trade routes, which were then dominated by Portuguese and Arab traders. From here, the spread into Africa, Europe, India and the Far East would have been quite rapid, with each region growing their own varieties.

Today, some of the finest (and hottest) chillies in the world are grown in Britain by farmers with a passion for the fiery fruit! Peoples thirst for more and more heat has increased as they get used to a certain level of chilli and then want more.

SCOVILLE SCALE

The heat of chilli is measured using a method known as the Scoville Scale.

Created by a scientist named Wilbur Scoville, who sported a rather fetching moustache, it is the world's unofficial chilli heat rating system. Opposite is a chart describing different chillies and their heat levels:

Mr Singh's Fabulous Fiery Cookbook

15,000,000-16,000,000	**PURE CAPSAICIN**
2,000,000-5,300,000	**PEPPER SPRAY**
1,400,000-2,300,000	**CAROLINA REAPER**
1,200,000-2,000,000	**TRINIDAD SCORPION**
1,200,000-2,000,000	**GHOST PEPPER**
425,000-577,000	**CHOCOLATE HABANERO**
350,000-577,000	**RED SAVINA**
100,000-350,000	**HABANERO**
100,000-350,000	**SCOTCH BONNET**
50,000-100,000	**THAI PEPPER**
50,000-100,000	**CHILTEPIN**
50,000-100,000	**MALAGUETA PEPPER**
40,000-60,000	**PEQUIN PEPPER**
30,000-50,000	**TABASCO PEPPER**
30,000-50,000	**SERRANO PEPPER**
5,000-10,000	**HUNGARIAN WAX**
2,500-8,000	**JALAPENO PEPPER**
1,500-2,500	**ROCOTILLO PEPPER**
1,000-1,500	**POBLANO PEPPER**
500-2,500	**ANAHEIM PEPPER**
100-500	**PIMENTO PEPPER**
100-500	**PEPERONCINI**
0	**BELL PEPPER**

MEET THE FAMILY

Mr Singh's is very much a family run business and its success is testament to the hard work, commitment and imagination of our close-knit team. Every member of the Singh clan brings something special and unique to the table and in this book the whole family has got involved to share their favourite recipes with you. Before we do, we wanted to take the time to introduce ourselves and tell you a bit about our chilli-led dreams.

MR SINGH (AKA POPS)

Ever since I was a child I have been driven by a desire to succeed and be seen as successful. I first trained as a product designer, but have also dabbled in many other arenas to find my niche. Sometimes you can't see what's right in front of you, and in my youth I would never have guessed that it would be my love of spicy food and cooking that would open the path to my destiny.

I have always love chilli and chilli sauces and had amassed quite a collection before I tried to make my own. I found that most of the store-bought sauces were either too sweet and lacked heat, or so hot that they masked all flavour, which is why I decided to try to make my own for a family barbecue back in 1985. At that time I was working as a chef and caterer and would often serve my chilli sauce at events. It wasn't long before customers were asking if they could buy bottles of the sauce to take home, which was the first spark that I might be able to combine my love of chilli with a successful business – the rest is history!

I am very proud of the business that my family and I have worked to create and that I have been able to share this journey with them. Today, I take on the role of Creative and Sales Director at the company, developing new recipes and building up our client base. We've come a long way since first bottling our sauces in our garden shed and I am so excited to see where our journey takes us next!

MUM (AKA MAMA SINGH)

Wife to Pops and mother to three wonderful sons, I couldn't be prouder of my family.

I feel that the values of my upbringing as a loving daughter, sister, wife, daughter-in-law and mother are all bottled up in Mr Singh's Sauces which makes me so proud that my children have made this beautiful business work, achieved their goals and made their father's dream come true.

My family keeps me motivated and I am always happy to lend my time and my kitchen to create new recipes. I may be in the background at times but am always involved in some way which makes our business thrive and brings us together as a family.

KULDIP

I like to think of myself as a dreamer and creator. I am the business brains of the outfit and am responsible for leading Mr Singh's to where it is today from our humble beginnings in my parent's shed!

I love being in love (with Amar, my wife, who I still introduce her as my girlfriend!). I love discovering delicious new foods and exploring the wonders of the world. I am quite geeky about Lego, dinosaurs and art and design. I also love to read books about history, leadership, philosophy, spirituality, biography and business.

I love to expand my horizons and try new experiences whenever they I get the opportunity. Interestingly, I once took a listening course with an ex Scotland Yard hostage negotiator!

I love my huge (extended) family. I am blessed to have grown up in a house full of laughter. I have always been surrounded by uncles, aunts, cousins, grandparents, siblings and parents who have all enriched my life.

AMAR

Hi, I'm Amar! I am Kuldip's wife. I am an adventurer who has been lucky enough to explore the world. I want to fill my life with love, culture and generosity. I'm often told that I am full of energy and the 'life of a party'. I enjoy healthy, clean and green food which tastes delicious and fills me with energy. I also adore tasty wine and great company. My philosophy in life is: Life is too short not to eat chocolate.

RAV

I am Rav – the middle child, wrestling fanatic, chilli addict, too hot to handle, too cold to hold, beard growing, tattoo getting, styling and profiling, chilli sauce eating, BMW driving, son of my mum ... husband to Sonia and daddy of baby Neev.

Mr Singh's Fabulous Fiery Cookbook

SONIA

I am chatty, smiley, wife to Rav and mummy to baby Neev. I love fitness, cooking and find cleaning weirdly therapeutic! I helped with invoicing when Mr Singh's first started out and perfected my chilli-sauce sales pitch when we first started selling at exhibitions.

SUKHI (AKA BUTCH)

Hello, my name is Sukhi but everyone calls me Butch.

I am the youngest of the Singh sons. I am a gym addict, food fanatic and a big fan of piercings and tattoos. I like to dress well and look good, which makes me question why I always end up with food all over my clothes and face? I really hope you all like the book – my recipes represent me by being fun, tasty and hot! (The chillies I mean.)

BREAKFASTS

EGG AND BACON WRAP WITH PUNJABI PESTO

AMAR: This is a Sunday morning favourite in our house, especially if we've overdone it on the Saturday night. If you prepare the dough in advance, it's quick to make, filling and delicious. Plus, it's got just enough heat to knock the cobwebs from between your ears and have you ready to face the day. These wraps are also great portable food, so we always have a few on hand for Singh family roadtrips. Perfect with a mug of Granny Singh's Punjabi Tea (see page 36).

PREPARATION TIME: 5 MINUTES
COOKING TIME: 15 MINUTES

Serves 4

4 Paratha (see page 144)

12 rashers streaky bacon

4 eggs

2 tbsp milk

1 tsp salt

1 tsp garam masala

1 tsp chilli powder

1 tbsp ghee or vegetable oil, for frying

8 tbsp Mr Singh's Punjabi Pesto or Thurka (see page 152)

Preheat the grill (broiler) to medium.

Make the Paratha as per the recipe on page 144 and set aside.

Lay the bacon flat on a grill pan and place under the grill for 10–15 minutes, until really crunchy, turning halfway through cooking.

While the bacon is cooking make the omelettes. For each omelette, beat 1 egg with ½ tablespoon of milk, ¼ teaspoon salt, ¼ tsp garam masala and ¼ tsp chilli powder. Heat some of the ghee or vegetable oil in a small frying pan or skillet over a medium heat then pour in the egg mixture. Cook for 2 minutes, until the omelette is firm then turn out onto a plate. Set aside and keep warm while you make the remaining omelettes.

To assemble, place the paratha on to serving plates and spread each with 2 tablespoons Mr Singh's Punjabi Pesto or Thurka. Lay one of the omelettes over each flatbread and top each omelette with 3 rashers of the streaky bacon.

Eat straight away or roll in foil to eat later. Serve with a steaming mug of Granny Singh's Punjabi Tea (see page 36) and a smile on your face.

CHILLI AND HAM CROISSANT

AMAR: Whilst Kuldip and I were enjoying a weekend away in Paris, we got to know the local baker and decided to use his wares to create a Singh-style breakfast. I know that it's risky to mess with the classics, but these delicious morsels are creamy, crispy, buttery, salty, spicy and sweet all in one bite. Delicious with a cup of strong black coffee.

PREPARATION TIME: 10 MINUTES
COOKING TIME: 10 MINUTES

Serves 4

25 g/1 oz unsalted butter

1 tsp garlic powder

200 g/7 oz baby spinach

4 plain croissants, sliced in
  half lengthways

8 slices good-quality ham,
  sliced in half

200 g/7 oz/scant 2 cups grated
  Cheddar cheese

1 tsp chilli powder (or to taste)

4 eggs

salt and freshly ground pepper

Preheat the grill (broiler) to high.

Melt the butter in a frying pan or skillet over a medium heat, then add the garlic powder and stir to combine. When the butter just starts to brown add the spinach to the pan and stir to coat in the butter. Cook for 5 minutes, stirring continuously, until the spinach has wilted. Transfer the spinach to a plate and cover. Set aside. Keep the pan and any remaining juices in it to hand as you will need them again later.

Lay the croissant halves, open side up, on a grill pan and place under the grill until just golden, about 2 minutes. Transfer to a wire rack to cool. Do not switch the grill off.

Once your croissants have cooled slightly, place half a slice of ham on each piece of croissant. Spoon the cooked spinach over the ham, sharing it out evenly between the pieces. Sprinkle the grated cheese over the top of the spinach and then season with the salt and chilli powder, adding enough chilli to satisfy your appetite for heat.

Return the pan that you cooked the spinach in to the heat, adding more butter if necessary, and crack the eggs into the pan. Cook them sunny-side up until the whites are set but the yolks are still runny. Season the eggs with salt, pepper and any remaining chilli powder.

Meanwhile, place the bottom halves of the croissants back on to the grill pan and place under the grill for a couple of minutes, until the cheese has melted and started to turn golden.

Divide the bottom halves of the croissants between 4 serving plates and top each with a fried egg. Carefully flip the croissant tops over and place one on top of each of the eggs. Serve immediately.

Mr Singh's Fabulous Fiery Cookbook

PUNJABI PINNI BALLS

SONIA: Despite being sweet, these are actually really healthy and are even said to boost the immune system. In fact, after my son, Neev, was born I was given a three month supply and used to enjoy a couple every morning alongside a cup of turmeric-infused milk. They are a labour of love as they need to be stirred continuously over a very low heat for the duration of cooking, so get yourself a cup of tea, put on the radio and settle in for a bit of an arm workout.

PREPARATION TIME: 45 MINUTES
COOKING TIME: 90 MINUTES

Makes about 80

100 g/3½ oz/½ cup dried mung beans

50 g/1¾ oz/½ cup fennel seeds

80 g/3 oz/½ cup linseeds (flax seeds)

70 g/2½ oz/½ cup dried pumpkin seeds

200 g/7 oz/scant 1¾ cups shelled pistachio nuts

650 g/1 lb 7 oz/3 cups ghee

125 g/4½ oz/1 cup atta or wholemeal flour

125 g/4½ oz/1 cup gram (chickpea) flour

175 g/6 oz/1 cup coarse semolina

600 g/1 lb 5 oz/3½ cups ground almonds

300 g/10½ oz/2 cups powdered palm sugar (jaggery)

70 g/2½ oz/½ cup green sultanas (golden raisins)

First, prepare your spices. Place the mung beans in a dry frying pan or skillet over a low heat and toast until starting to turn golden brown. Transfer to a spice or coffee grinder and grind to a smooth powder. Pass the powder through a sieve (strainer) to remove any unground pieces and set aside in a small bowl. Repeat this process with the fennel seeds, linseeds (flax seeds) and pumpkin seeds, placing each spice in a separate bowl. The pistachio nuts also need to be ground to a powder, but do not toast them first.

Once you have prepared all of your spices, you are ready to start cooking. Place the ghee in a large pan over a low heat. Once the ghee has melted, turn the heat right down and add the atta or wholemeal flour to the pan and cook, stirring continuously, for 20 minutes. Add the gram (chickpea) flour and cook, still stirring, for 15 minutes. Add the semolina and continue to stir over the heat for another 15 minutes, then add the ground mung beans and stir over the heat for another 15 minutes. Now add the ground fennel seeds and stir until you see the ghee start to rise to the top of the pan. Add the linseeds and cook, still stirring, for another 10 minutes, then add the pumpkin seeds and cook for 5 minutes more. The mixture will have started to look quite dry by now, but don't worry about this as it is necessary to form the balls after the mixture is cooked.

Add the ground almonds and pistachios to the pan and stir over heat for 3 further minutes, then remove the pan from the heat. Finally, stir the palm sugar (jaggery) and green sultanas (golden raisins) through the mixture. Set the mixture aside until cool enough to handle, then use your hands to roll the mixture into golf ball-sized balls. Place the balls on a sheet of baking parchment and set aside to cool completely.

Serve a couple of these balls per person with a cup of tea or glass of milk for breakfast. They will keep for three months in an airtight container.

GRANNY SINGH'S SPICY SCRAMBLED EGGS

KULDIP: Health and fitness is always a big topic at Singh family gatherings, and when it comes to the gym we're not afraid to get a little competitive. My brothers and I often tease each other about who has the biggest biceps, my father wants a body like Bruce Lee and my wife, Amar, is always eating delicious, healthy food to stay slim. One bright Sunday morning (after a blurry Saturday night), I was inspired by all the delicious looking healthy food that was clogging up my Instagram feed and decided to make a 'clean', filling breakfast and turned to Granny Singh for help. She came up with this gem – it involves almost no cooking and minimal preparation.

PREPARATION TIME: 5 MINUTES
COOKING TIME: 10 MINUTES

Serves 4

6 eggs

1½ tbsp milk

2 ripe avocados

4 slices pumpernickel bread

4 medium sized tomatoes, finely chopped

1 onion, finely chopped

6 slices good-quality ham, sliced into thin strips

25 g/1 oz unsalted butter

150 g/5½ oz Mr Singh's Punjabi Pesto or Thurka (see page 152)

salt and freshly ground pepper, to season

Crack the eggs into a large bowl and add the milk. Beat the mixture together, season with salt and pepper and set aside.

Halve the avocados and discard the stones. Remove the flesh from the skins and place in a bowl. Mash the avocado flesh roughly with the back of a fork and spread the mixture over the slices of pumpernickel bread, dividing it evenly between the slices.

In another bowl, combine the tomatoes, onion and ham and mix together. Spoon this mixture over the avocado-topped bread and season with salt and pepper.

To make the scrambled eggs, melt the butter in a large pan over medium heat. Add the Mr Singh's Punjabi Pesto or Thurka and stir until heated through. Pour the egg mixture into the pan and cook, stirring continuously, until the eggs are scrambled to your liking.

Divide the topped pumpernickel between 4 serving plates and spoon the eggs over the top, dividing them evenly between the plates. Serve immediately.

SPICED EGGY BREAD WITH CHILLI SAUCE

KULDIP: We loved this bread when we were young children, mum used to make it on rainy days when we would all gather in the kitchen to listen to the rain pouring down. Despite these fond childhood memories, the spices here give this eggy bread a distinctly more grown-up flavour than more traditional versions. I like mine slathered in chilli sauce, but you can use a much, or as little, as you like.

PREPARATION TIME: 5 MINUTES

COOKING TIME: 10 MINUTES

Serves 5

7 eggs

10 slices white bread

½ tsp salt

½ tsp chilli powder

1 fresh green finger chilli, finely chopped

½ tsp garam masala

2 tsp milk

1 handful finely chopped coriander (cilantro) leaves

2 tbsp vegetable oil, for frying

Mr Singh's Hot Punjabi Chilli Sauce or Basic Chilli Sauce (see page 150), to serve

Break the eggs into a large mixing bowl and beat to combine. Add the salt, chilli powder, fresh chilli, garam masala, milk and most of the coriander (cilantro) to the bowl and mix to combine.

Place a large frying pan or skillet over a medium heat and add the oil. Once the oil is hot, take a slice of the bread and dip it into the egg mixture to thoroughly coat. Place the bread into the hot pan and leave to cook for around 40 seconds, then carefully flip the bread to cook the other side for another 40 seconds.

Transfer the bread to a warm plate lined with kitchen paper while you repeat the process for the remaining slices.

Once all the bread is cooked, divide the slices between 5 serving plates and sprinkle with the remaining coriander. Serve with chilli sauce on the side.

Mr Singh's Fabulous Fiery Cookbook

PUNJABI PAPRIKA PORRIDGE

KULDIP: When my brothers and I went to stay with our grandmother as children, she would make this healthy, warming breakfast on cold winter mornings. The recipe has grown and developed as we have, and we all have our own magic formula to making our individual versions of the perfect Punjabi porridge. The version listed below is my favourite (and the best!), but, in Singh family tradition, feel free to tweak it to your own personal tastes.

PREPARATION TIME: 25 MINUTES
COOKING TIME: 45 MINUTES

Serves 4

4 tsp ghee

2 tsp sweet paprika

2 tsp ground cinnamon

4 tsp chopped almonds

4 tsp chopped pistachio nuts, plus extra to garnish

200 g/7 oz/generous 1¼ cups jumbo rolled or steel cut oats

1 litre/1¾ pints/generous 4 cups milk

4 tsp honey

Warm the ghee in a large pan over a medium heat. Add the paprika, cinnamon, almonds and pistachios and stir to coat in the ghee. Cook for 1 minute, until the spices are fragrant.

Add the oats to the pan and stir to coat in the spices. Pour in the milk and 200 ml/⅓ pint/generous ¾ cup water and stir to combine. Bring the mixture to a simmer, then turn the heat down to low and cook for 5 minutes, until the oats have softened.

Divide the cooked porridge between 4 serving bowls and drizzle a teaspoon of honey over each. Serve hot, garnished with extra pistachios.

POORI (DEEP-FRIED ROTI)

MAMA SINGH: These make a great weekend brunch, especially when the boys and their families are all home and they have had a big night the evening before. I get up early and prepare these, then begin frying them off at about 11am, the delicious smell wafts up the stairs and brings the family staggering down from their beds.

PREPARATION TIME: 30 MINUTES

COOKING TIME: 10 MINUTES

Makes 20

250 g/9 oz/generous 2 cups wholewheat flour, plus extra for dusting

pinch of salt

2 tbsp milk

7 tbsp water

1 litre/1¾ pints vegetable or sunflower oil, for frying

Place the flour and salt in a large mixing bowl and create a well in the centre. Pour the milk and water into the well and bring together to form a firm dough. Turn the dough on to a lightly floured surface and knead for around 10 minutes, until firm and pliable. Set aside for 10 minutes.

Knead the dough a second time for around 5 minutes, then divide into 20 equal-sized pieces, rolling each piece into a ball with the cupped palms of your hands.

Place the oil in a deep-fat fryer or large wok and heat to 180°C/350°F, or until a dropped piece of dough immediately rises to the surface and fries to a nice golden brown. It is important that the oil is at the right temperature as otherwise your poori will be undercooked and greasy.

While the oil is heating, roll the balls of dough out to form 4 cm/1½ in rounds. Working with 2 or 3 rounds of dough at a time, carefully drop them into the oil and gently pat them until they start to puff up.

Fry for 20 seconds on one side, then flip over and fry for an additional 20 seconds. The poori should be golden brown and nicely puffed up. Transfer the cooked breads to kitchen roll to drain while you continue to cook the remaining poori.

Serve immediately, brushed with ghee for breakfast or alongside a vegetable curry for a light meal.

HONEY AND YOGURT

AMAR: Spring has to be my favourite time of year, especially when you start to get great English strawberries and blackberries. I love this snack at any time of day, and, despite it being in the breakfast chapter, am as likely to have it last thing at night as first thing in the morning. It takes 5 minutes to prepare and is deliciously fresh and filling.

PREPARATION TIME: 5 MINUTES
COOKING TIME: N/A

Serves 1

125 ml/4 fl oz/ /½ cup low-fat
  natural yogurt
generous handful mixed nuts
generous handful fresh mixed
  berries (I like strawberries
  and blueberries)
1 pinch cinnamon
1 tbsp runny honey

Place half of the yogurt in a serving bowl and sprinkle over half of the nuts, berries, cinnamon and honey.

Repeat layering with the second half of the ingredients and serve immediately.

GRANNY SINGH'S PUNJABI TEA

KULDIP: Of all the recipes in this book, this was the first that I made myself. When I was 8, my gran was visiting from her home in Kenya and was filling our home with the fragrant aroma of her delicious tea. My brothers and I had all grown up with this tea and loved it, so I was keen to learn how to make it myself. My gran didn't use anything as precise as measuring spoons as for her the process was much more organic and she would weigh the spices in her hand to get the right balance before adding them. She also had a sweet tooth and would always add at least two teaspoons of sugar to her cup, but I've left that out here as I prefer it without (feel free to add your own though!)

PREPARATION TIME: 5 MINUTES

COOKING TIME: 10 MINUTES

Serves 4

850 ml/1½ pints/generous 3½ cups cold water

1 tsp fennel seeds

3 green cardamom pods

1 tsp caraway seeds

4 teabags

sugar, to taste

250 ml/9 fl oz/generous 1 cup milk

Put the water and spices into a large pan and slowly bring to the boil. Once boiling, reduce the heat to a gentle simmer, add the teabags and leave to steep for a couple of minutes.

Add the milk and bring the tea back to the boil for 2 minutes. Strain the tea into mugs and serve hot, offering the sugar alongside.

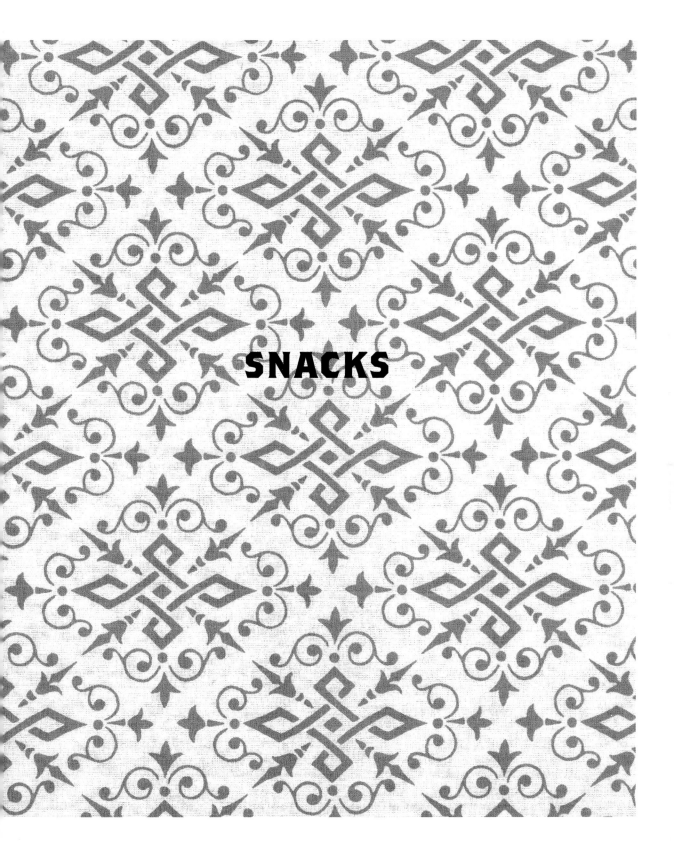

SNACKS

CHILLI CHICKEN WINGS

POPS: These wings are sticky, moreish and VERY spicy. My boys love them and are sure to turn up to a party at our family home if they hear that 'Pops is making chicken wings!' If you aren't a fan of very hot food then feel free to temper the spice to suit your own tastes.

PREPARATION TIME: 5 MINUTES
COOKING TIME: 20 MINUTES

Serves 4

2 tbsp vegetable oil

1 tsp red chilli powder

12 skinless chicken niblets or small drumsticks

1 bottle Mr Singh's Hot Punjabi Chilli Sauce or 1 quantity Basic Chilli Sauce (see page 151)

½ bunch fresh coriander (cilantro), leaves chopped, to garnish

Heat the oil in a large pan or casserole over a medium heat. Once hot, add the chilli powder to the oil and stir to combine.

Increase the heat to high then add the chicken to the pan and cook, stirring continuously, for 3–5 minutes, until the chicken skin is sealed and has started to turn golden. Lower the heat to medium then pour in the chilli sauce and stir to ensure the chicken is well coated. Bring to a simmer and cook the chicken for 15 minutes, until the meat is cooked through and the sauce is reduced and thickened to a thick paste.

If the sauce is too liquid, remove the chicken from the pan and continue to cook the sauce until you are happy with the consistency. Returning the chicken to the pan once the sauce has thickened.

Turn the chicken wings on to a serving plate and serve garnished with fresh chopped coriander (cilantro).

POP'S CUMIN CHICKEN

POPS: Though a product designer by trade, I used to moonlight as a chef at various East African/Indian members clubs in London. At one of these, Gymkhana on Green Lane, I developed this recipe that often caused queues round the block. Years later, this is still a firm family favourite and a great dish for celebrations.

PREPARATION TIME: 5 MINUTES
COOKING TIME: 30 MINUTES

Serves 4

3 tbsp mustard oil
4 onions, finely chopped
25 g/1 oz cumin Seeds
8 skinless chicken niblets
1 tbsp salt
1 tsp chilli powder
1 tsp chopped green finger chillies
1 tbsp ground cumin
1 tsp tamarind concentrate
1 tsp runny honey
1 tsp lime juice
½ bunch fresh coriander (cilantro), leaves chopped

Heat the oil over a medium flame in a large pan, then add the onions and cook, stirring continuously, until soft and just starting to turn brown, around 5 minutes. Add the cumin seeds to the pan and continue to cook, still stirring, until the onions are nicely golden.

Reduce the heat to low and add all the remaining ingredients, except the lime juice and coriander (cilantro), to the pan. Stir everything together then set aside to cook, stirring occasionally, for around 15 minutes, until the chicken has cooked through.

Once the chicken is cooked through, turn off the heat and stir in the lime juice and chopped coriander (cilantro). Serve hot, eating with your hands.

MR SINGH'S SAUSAGES

KULDIP: Desperately hunting round the kitchen for something to eat one day and coming up with only a pack of sausages and a jar of our barbecue sauce, I decided to throw caution to the wind and cook them up together. Miraculously, the result was delicious - the fat from the sausages seeping into the sauce and making it really unctuous and sticky.

PREPARATION TIME: 10 MINUTES
COOKING TIME: 25 MINUTES

Serves 4

8 sausages of your choice
1 jar of Mr Singh's Chilli Barbecue Sauce or 1 quantity Thurka (see page 152)
½ bunch fresh coriander (cilantro), leaves chopped

Preheat the grill (broiler) to high and line a grill pan with foil.

Cook the sausages under the grill, turning occassionally, until cooked through, around 15 minutes. Transfer to a chopping board and slice into 2.5 cm/½ in discs.

Place the barbecue sauce or Thurka into a medium pan with 100 ml/3½ fl oz/scant 1 cup water and heat to a gentle simmer. Add the sausages and stir through the sauce to coat.

Add another 400 ml/14 fl oz/generous 1½ cups of water to the pan and leave to cook for 10 minutes until bubbling and starting to thicken. If the sauce is too thick, add a little more water.

Stir in the chopped coriander (cilantro) and serve warm. For a more substantial meal, serve with rice, chapatis or salad.

KENYAN KEBAB

POPS: This dish transports me back to the days of my youth, growing up in East Africa – a time of my life that I remember very fondly as, to me at least, it seemed like everyone got on and there was a real sense of community. These kebabs, served directly off the skewer, are another dish that my sons expect at every family barbecue, and I am only too happy to oblige.

PREPARATION TIME: 30 MINUTES

COOKING TIME: 15 MINUTES

Serves 4

2 onions, finely chopped

thumb-size piece fresh ginger, finely chopped

5 garlic cloves, finely chopped

2 green bird's-eye chillies, finely sliced

2 tsp red chilli powder

1 tsp salt

2 tsp garam masala

1 large handful fresh coriander (cilantro), leaves chopped

500 g/1 lb 2 oz minced (ground) lamb (approx. 20% fat)

bread rolls and chilli sauce, to serve (optional)

Place all of the ingredients except the lamb into a large bowl and mix together to ensure everything is evenly distributed. Now, add the lamb to the mixture and use your hands to combine everything together, squeezing the meat to ensure that all of the ingredients are evenly distributed. Once you are happy with the mixture, use your knuckles to compress it into the bowl, cover with clingfilm (plastic wrap) and set aside to rest in the refrigerator for 20 minutes.

To cook under the grill (broiler):
Preheat the grill (broiler) to high and line a grill pan with foil.

Divide the mixture into 4 equal-size portions and roll into balls with your hands. Flatten each ball into a patty no thicker than 1 cm/½ in, then place under the grill and cook for 5–8 minutes, then flip them over and cook for an additional 5 minutes on the other side. Serve with bread rolls and chilli sauce on the side.

To cook on the charcoal barbecue (grill):
To cook these over charcoal, you need a barbecue and 4 square-shaped metal skewers. Add lumpwood charcoal and lighting fluid to the barbecue and ignite the charcoal. Once the coals are red hot, let them settle until they are no longer glowing.

Divide the mixture into 4 equal-size portions and roll into balls with your hands. Now take a skewer and feed it through the centre of one of the balls, using your hands to squeeze the kebab onto the centre of the skewer and creating a long sausage shape, approximately 15 cm/6 in long. Repeat with the remaining kebabs.

Place the kebabs over the prepared coals and cook, turning occassionally, for 15 minutes, until cooked through. Serve immediately with chilli sauce on the side.

CHEESE-STUFFED MEATBALLS 🔥🔥

BUTCH: These meatballs are a no-brainer for me; meaty, gooey and cheesey – all of my favourite types of food in one bite-sized mouthful! They are a great addition to any picnic, barbecue or summer party.

PREPARATION TIME: 30 MINUTES
COOKING TIME: 10 MINUTES

Serves 4

100 g/3½ oz/generous ¾ cup plain (all-purpose) flour

1 tsp turmeric

4 tsp chilli powder

4 eggs

500 g/1 lb 2 oz minced (ground) beef

½ onion, finely chopped

1 tsp ground turmeric

1 tsp garam masala

2 tsp salt

100 g/3½ oz Cheddar cheese, cut into 4 even cubes

2 tbsp sunflower oil, for frying

Mr Singh's BBQ Chilli Sauce, to serve (optional)

Place the flour, turmeric and 2 teaspoons of the chilli powder into a small bowl. Beat the eggs into another bowl and set on the worktop next to the first bowl.

Place the minced (ground) beef, onion, turmeric, garam masala, the remaining chilli powder and salt in a large bowl and use your hands to ensure that everything is evenly distributed throughout the mix.

Divide the meat mixture into 4 equal-size balls then, working with one ball at a time, flatten in the palm of your hand and place a cube of cheese in the centre. Enclose your hand to seal the cheese within the meat, then rotate in the palms of your cupped hands to form a nice ball shape that is firmly sealed. Repeat with the remaining three meatballs.

Roll the balls in the flour mixture you prepared earlier then dunk into the egg mixture to coat then finally back into the flour mixture. Place the meatballs in the fridge for 20 minutes to rest.

Heat the oil in a large frying pan or skillet, then add the meatballs to the pan and cook, turning occasionally, for 10 minutes, until cooked through and golden brown on the outside.

Serve hot with Mr Singh's Barbecue Sauce alongside for dipping.

POP'S SPECIALTY FLAT CHIPS 🔥🔥

POPS: These crispy morsels are almost like a battered chip and need to be eaten straight away for maximum crunch. In Kenya these are known as *Maru Bhajiya*, named after the restaurant that first served them. These are delicious served with mint or chilli sauce on the side – be prepared to get addicted!

PREPARATION TIME: 5 MINUTES
COOKING TIME: 10 MINUTES

Serves 4

6 tbsp gram (chickpea) flour
1 tbsp salt
2 tbsp red chilli powder
12 medium white potatoes or 6 large, cut into 3 mm/¼ in slices
1–2 litres mustard oil, for frying

Place the gram (chickpea) flour, salt and chilli powder into a small bowl and mix together to combine with your hands.

Place the potato slices in a large bowl and sprinkle the flour and spice mixture over, mix everything with your hands to ensure the slices are evenly coated. Set aside for 5 minutes to allow the spice mixture to draw out any liquid from the potatoes, then, adding only a little at a time, slowly pour in water to create a thick batter. You are looking for a thick, creamy texture that easily coats the surface of the potatoes.

In a large pan or deep-fat fryer, heat the oil to 180°C/350°F, or until a dropped slice of potato immediately rises to the surface and fries to a nice golden brown. Once the oil is at temperature, start adding the potato slices carefully to the oil one by one. The best method is to scrape the batter from the sides of the bowl with a potato in your hand and use your thumb to spread the batter over the surface of the potato before inserting in the oil.

After 2 minutes the potato slices should be golden brown and crispy, transfer to kitchen paper to drain while you continue to cook the remaining slices.

Serve plain or with your choice of dipping sauce.

Mr Singh's Fabulous Fiery Cookbook

MOZZARELLA STICKS

BUTCH: Confession time ... Though I grew up in a family with a strong food culture that is embedded in Indian and Kenyan cuisine, my real food passion is American-style fast food. These gooey mozzarella sticks are no exception, though I have given them a Mr Singh's spicy twist. You might need to push a bit harder at the gym after a few of these, but, for me at least, they're totally worth it.

PREPARATION TIME: 20 MINUTES, PLUS FREEZING

COOKING TIME: 5 MINUTES

Serves 4

150 g/5½ oz firm mozzarella (get the kind that is sold in blocks to use on pizza)

6 slices slightly stale white bread

1 tbsp chilli powder

1 tbsp ground turmeric

2 tbsp salt

2 tbsp garam masala

3 eggs, beaten

200 g/7 oz/generous 1½ cups plain (all-purpose) flour

1–2 litres/1¾–2½ pints vegetable oil, for frying

Mr Singh's Chilli Barbecue Sauce, to serve (optional)

Slice the cheese into 1 cm-/½ in-thick batons and set aside.

Place the bread in a food processor and pulse to fine breadcrumbs. Add the chilli powder, turmeric, salt and garam masala to the processor and pulse again. Transfer the seasoned breadcrumbs to a bowl.

Prepare your work surface by lining up your bowls of flour, beaten eggs and seasoned breadcrumbs next to each other. The key to making these really crunchy is to 'double dip' the cheese in the breadcrumbs. Working with one at a time, take a cheese baton and coat it in the flour, then dip immediately into the egg and then into the breadcrumbs to coat. Now return the coated mozzarella stick to the egg and then finally back into the breadcrumbs a second time to create a double coating. Place the coated sticks on a plate or chopping board while you continue with the rest.

Once all of your sticks are coated, place them in the freezer to firm up for a minimum of 1 hour 30 minutes – this helps to ensure that the cheese doesn't melt too quickly in the hot oil.

When you are ready to cook, heat the oil to 180°C/350°F in a large pan or deep-fat fryer (if using a deep-fat fryer, use the amount of oil that the manufacturer recommends). Working in batches of 3, carefully drop the mozzarella sticks into the hot oil and fry until golden and crispy on the outside and gooey in the centre. This will take between 30 seconds and 1 minute. Set aside to drain any excess oil on kitchen paper while you cook the others.

Serve the mozzarella sticks hot with Mr Singh's Chilli Barbecue Sauce alongside.

Mr Singh's Fabulous Fiery Cookbook

POHA (RICE FLAKES)

MAMA SINGH: *Poha* (sometimes sold as flaked, flattened or beaten rice) is rice that has been parboiled then rolled to create flakes. The larger surface area of the flakes means that they absorbs flavours really well, which makes this perfect for mid-afternoon snack time when you're craving something spicy or salty to get you through till dinner.

PREPARATION TIME: 5 MINUTES
COOKING TIME: 20 MINUTES

Serves 4

2 tbsp vegetable oil

½ tsp cumin seeds

½ tsp black mustard seeds

2 garlic cloves, crushed

125 g/4½ oz/¾ cup frozen sweetcorn

1 onion, finely chopped

1 green bird's-eye chilli, finely chopped

¼ tsp ground turmeric

200 g/7 oz/scant 1 cup flaked rice (poha), washed

salt and freshly ground pepper

small bunch chopped fresh coriander (cilantro), to garnish

Place the oil over a medium heat in a large pan. Once hot, add the cumin seeds, mustard seeds and crushed garlic to the pan and cook, stirring continuously, until fragrant and the mustard seeds are just starting to pop, around 2 minutes.

Add the sweetcorn, onion and chilli to the pan and stir to coat in the spices. Turn the heat to low and cook, stirring occasionally, for 5 minutes.

Add the turmeric and flaked rice (poha) to the pan and season with salt and pepper. Cook the mixture, stirring continuously, for 2 minutes then remove the pan from the heat and cover. Set aside for 10 minutes for the rice to finish cooking, then spoon into a serving bowl and garnish with the coriander (cilantro). Serve hot.

CRUNCHY PEA BALLS

MAMA SINGH: My mother-in-law taught me how to make these crunchy morsels that are a firm family favourite and make a great pre-dinner snack to enjoy with drinks. She always bought fresh peas and froze them herself as she had a firmly ingrained distrust of any store-bought frozen vegetable!

PREPARATION TIME: 5 MINUTES
COOKING TIME: 15 MINUTES

Makes 16

300 g/10½ oz/2 cups
    frozen peas
100 g/3½ oz/generous 1 cup
    gram (chickpea bean) flour
3 garlic cloves, crushed
thumb-size piece fresh ginger,
    finely chopped
2 green finger chillies,
    finely chopped
1 tsp salt
½ tsp ajwain seeds
1 litre/1¾ pints vegetable or
    sunflower oil, for frying
Mr Singh's Punjabi Pesto
    or ½ quantity Thurka (see
    page 152), to serve (optional)

Place the peas in colander and run them briefly under a hot tap to de-ice them. Place them in a blender and blitz until almost smooth – I like to leave a few pea halves in the mixture for texture.

Place the pea puree in a large bowl along with the gram (chickpea bean) flour, garlic, ginger, chillies, salt and ajwain seeds. Mix well with your hands to combine, the mixture should be sticky and quite firm.

Place the oil in a large frying pan or skillet and heat to 180°C/350°F, or until a teaspoon of the mixture immediately rises to the surface and fries to a golden brown.

Place a bowl of water on your worktop next to the pea mixture. Using your hands, form the pea mixture into golf ball-sized balls, dipping your hands in the water between forming each one. There should be enough mixture to make 16 balls.

Working in 2 batches, carefully place the balls in the hot oil and leave to cook for 6–8 minutes, until they rise to float on the surface of the oil and have turned golden brown. You will need to move the balls around in the pan from time to time during cooking to prevent them from sticking to the base of your pan. Place the balls on a plate lined with kitchen towel to drain of any excess oil while you cook the remainder.

Serve the balls hot with Mr Singh's Punjabi Pesto or Thurka (see page 152) for dipping.

BOONDI YOGURT

MAMA SINGH: Boondi are tiny teardrops of crisp fried batter that add a delicious chewy texture to a bowl of yogurt and elevate it to something much more substantial. You can make the boondi at home by dripping batter into hot oil through the holes in a slotted spoon, but because this is meant to be a quick snack I have opted for the store-bought version here.

PREPARATION TIME: 15 MINUTES
COOKING TIME: N/A

Serves 4

500 g/1 lb 2 oz/2 cups plain Greek yogurt

200 mls/7 fl oz/scant 1 cup whole milk

½ tsp salt

¼ tsp freshly ground black pepper

¼ tsp garam masala

70 g/2½ oz/½ cup dried boondi

1 handful fresh coriander (cilantro), chopped

Place the yogurt and milk in a large bowl and whisk until smooth. Add the salt, pepper, garam masala and chilli powder and whisk again to combine.

Place the boondi in another bowl and pour over boiling water to cover. Soak the boondi for 30 seconds then drain through a sieve (strainer) or colander. Add the boondi to the bowl of yogurt and stir to combine.

Divide the mixture between 4 serving bowls and garnish with the fresh coriander (cilantro). Leave the bowls to rest for 10 minutes before serving.

LASSI 3 WAYS

POPS: I developed a real taste for salty lassis during my time studying in India. They were often served on the busy trains and made for refreshing relief from the humid carriages. Below are recipes for salty, sweet and a fruity mango lassi. Try them all and decide which is your favourite.

PREPARATION TIME: 5 MINUTES

COOKING TIME: N/A

Serves 4

FOR THE LASSI BASE:

ice cubes

500 g/1 lb 2 oz/2 cups plain
    Greek yogurt

1 tsp cumin seeds

1 litre/1¾ pints/generous
    4 cups water

FOR A SALTY LASSI:

2 tbsp salt, or to taste

FOR A SWEET LASSI:

2 tbsp granulated sugar

¼ tsp caraway seeds

FOR A MANGO LASSI:

100 g/3½ oz fresh mango, cut
    into cubes

2 tbsp honey

fresh mint, to garnish

Fill 4 tall glasses with ice cubes and set aside. Place the remaining ingredients for the lassi base in a blender, along with the additional ingredients for the type of lassi that you are making. Blend until smooth.

Divide the lassi among the ice-filled glasses. If you are making a mango lassi, garnish each glass with a sprig of mint. Serve immediately.

LUNCHES &
LIGHT MEALS

SPICY CHICKEN COUSCOUS

AMAR: Though I grew up learning how to cook Indian food, I love experimenting with different ingredients to incorporate them into the meals that I make. Couscous is one of the ingredients that I enjoy cooking with as it is a great base for strong flavours and absorbs them while cooking. This makes a great midweek lunch or light dinner as it is quick to prepare. It can also be made ahead and enjoyed cold as a packed lunch for work.

PREPARATION TIME: 5 MINUTES
COOKING TIME: 20 MINUTES

Serves 4

1 tbsp olive oil

1 tbsp cayenne pepper

1 tbsp ground coriander

2 tbsp Mr Singh's Hot Punjabi Chilli Sauce or Basic Chilli Sauce (see page 150)

2 chicken breasts, cut into bite-sized chunks

2 large tomatoes, roughly chopped

1 tsp salt

200 g/7 oz jarred roasted red (bell) peppers, roughly chopped

500 ml/18 fl oz/generous 2 cups chicken stock

250 g/9 oz/scant 1½ cups couscous

3 spring onions (scallions), finely sliced

1 handful fresh mint leaves, chopped, to garnish

1 lemon, quartered, to serve

Place a large pan over a medium heat and add the oil. Once the oil is hot, add the cayenne pepper, ground coriander and chilli sauce and cook for 1 minute, stirring continuously.

Add the chicken to the pan and stir to coat in the spices. Turn the heat to low and cook, stirring occasionally, for 10 minutes, until the chicken is almost cooked through.

Add the tomatoes, salt and chopped (bell) peppers to the pan, stir to combine then pour in the stock. Bring the stock back to a simmer, then pour in the couscous, stir once, cover and remove from the heat. Set the pan aside for 10 minutes for the couscous to absorb the stock and cook through.

Once cooked, use a fork to fluff up the couscous and separate the grains, then transfer the couscous into serving bowls. Scatter over the spring onions (scallions) and fresh mint and serve with lemon wedges alongside.

GRIDDLED CHICKEN AND VEGETABLES

AMAR: This is a great midweek meal or weekend lunch that has the added benefit that it helps you use up any leftover vegetables hiding at the back of your fridge at the end of the week. Feel free to adapt the recipe to include the ingredients that you have to hand. A really simple, tasty and healthy meal.

PREPARATION TIME: 10 MINUTES, PLUS MARINATING
COOKING TIME: 45 MINUTES

Serves 4

1 tbsp onion powder

1 tbsp paprika

1 tbsp dried thyme

½ tsp freshly ground black pepper

1 tbsp pink Himalayan salt

4 tbsp crème fraiche

4 chicken breasts

3 tbsp olive oil

1 courgette (zucchini), cut into 5 mm/¼ in batons

1 aubergine (eggplant), cut into 1 cm/½ slices

1 red (bell) pepper, cut into 2.5 cm/1 in wedges

1 red onion, cut into 1 cm/½ in slices

2 cooked beetroot (beets), cut into 5 mm/¼ in slices

Place the onion powder, paprika, dried thyme, pepper, salt and crème fraiche in a small bowl and stir to combine. Lay the chicken breasts flat in a small baking dish and pour over the sauce, using your hands to ensure that the chicken is well coated. Cover with clingfilm (plastic wrap) and place in the refrigerator to marinate for at least 30 minutes, this can be done up to a day ahead.

Place 1 tablespoon of the oil in a large heavy-based frying pan or skillet over a medium heat. Once hot, reduce the heat to low and lay the chicken breasts in the base of the pan. Cook for 10 minutes, then flip the chicken and cook for another 10 minutes on the other side. Remove the pan from the heat and add 100 ml/3½ fl oz/scant ½ cup boiling water, using the water to deglaze the pan. Cover the pan with a lid and set aside while you finish the vegetables.

Place a large griddle pan on hob over a high heat and leave to come to temperature for around 5 minutes. Place all of your prepared vegetables in a large mixing bowl and pour over the remaining olive oil. Give everything a mix with your hands to ensure that all the vegetables are lightly coated in the oil.

Once the griddle pan has come up to temperature reduce the heat to low then pick out the slices of aubergine from your bowl of vegetables and lay them on the pan. Cook for 5 minutes, then turn the aubergine slices and cook for 5 minutes more. Now lay the rest of the vegetables on the pan and cook for 15 minutes, turning halfway through, until all of the vegetables are tender.

Divide the vegetables between 4 serving plates and place 1 chicken breast on each plate. Spoon over any remaining sauce from the pan and serve warm.

EXTREMELY SPICY PIZZA

RAV: I've put this in the lunch chapter as it is a great dish for hungover Saturday mornings when you would typically reach for the pizza delivery menu. It has the added bonus of being knock-your-socks-off spicy, meaning that it should blow the headache right out of your ears! I first made this at a family party when someone new was being introduced. He asked me to make him something REALLY spicy and I duly obliged – he hasn't forgotten me (or the pizza) since! This version of the recipe is already toned down from the original, but if you're chilli averse then feel free to reduce the spice to suit your palate.

PREPARATION TIME: 25 MINUTES, PLUS RESTING
COOKING TIME: 10 MINUTES

Serves 4

FOR THE PIZZA DOUGH:

800 g/1lb 2 oz/scant 6½ cups plain (all-purpose) flour
10 g/¼ oz salt
2 tsp dried yeast
1 tbsp caster (superfine) sugar
3 tbsp olive oil

FOR THE TOMATO SAUCE:

6 tomatoes, roughly chopped
5 tbsp Mr Singh's Hot Punjabi Chilli Sauce or Basic Chilli Sauce (see page 150)
salt and freshly ground pepper

TO ASSEMBLE:

150 g/5½ oz/1 cup grated Cheddar cheese
Toppings of your choice – we like spinach, pepperoni, pineapple and ham

To make the pizza dough, sift the flour into a large bowl and add the salt, yeast and sugar. Make a well in the centre of the dough and pour in 600 ml/20 fl oz/2½ cups of lukewarm water and the olive oil. Using your hands, slowly start to incorporate the dry ingredients into the wet, until you have a sticky dough.

Lightly dust your work surface with flour and turn your dough out on to it. Knead the dough for 10 minutes until soft and springy. When you push your finger into the dough it should spring back. Lightly grease a large bowl with olive oil and transfer your dough to, covering it with a damp cloth. Set aside for 45 minutes, or until doubled in size.

While the dough is proving, make the tomato sauce. Place the tomatoes in a blender and pulse until smooth. Transfer to a bowl, add the chilli sauce and season to taste. Set aside until ready to use.

Preheat the oven to 240°C/475°F/gas mark 9 and preheat a large baking sheet or pizza stone. Once the dough has finished proving, lightly flour your work surface and tip your dough out on to it. Work the dough briefly with your hands to knock out any air pockets that have developed, then, using a rolling pin, roll out the pizza into a large round, approximately 30 cm/12 in.

Assemble your pizza by spreading it with tomato sauce then scattering over the grated cheese. Place your choice of toppings over the cheese and carefully transfer the pizza to the hot baking sheet or pizza stone. Transfer the pizza to the oven and bake for around 10 minutes, until the pizza is golden with a beautifully crisp crust. Slice into portions and serve hot.

SINGH-STYLE MEATBALLS

MAMA SINGH: When the boys were at school they would come home begging me to make the food that their friends had at home, and at the top of that list was pasta and meatballs! Being the dutiful mother I am, I created this recipe, which has all the trappings of the traditional Italian dish, but with a spicy Punjabi twist. The boys loved it!

PREPARATION TIME: 10 MINUTES
COOKING TIME: 45 MINUTES

Serves 4

FOR THE MEATBALLS:
250 g/9 oz minced pork
250 g/9 oz minced beef
1 tsp paprika
½ tsp garlic powder
1 tsp dried oregano
½ tsp salt
½ onion, finely chopped

FOR THE SAUCE:
2 tbsp olive oil
3 garlic cloves, crushed
1 onion, finely chopped
1 carrot, peeled and grated
500 g/1 lb 2 oz passata
1 x 400 g/14 oz tin chopped
  tomatoes
1½ tsp paprika
1 tsp mixed herbs
2 tbsp Mr Singh's Hot Punjabi
  Chilli Sauce or Basic Chilli
  Sauce (see page 150)
1 tsp salt
1 bunch fresh basil, to garnish

To make the meatballs, place all of the ingredients in a large bowl and mix together with your hands until thoroughly combined. Divide the mixture into 16 equal-sized balls and set aside until ready to cook.

To make the sauce, place the oil in a large pan over a medium heat. Once hot, add the garlic and chopped onion and cook, stirring continuously, until soft and just starting to turn golden, around 5 minutes.

Add the carrot to the pan and cook, stirring occasionally, until starting to soften, about 5 minutes. Add the passata and chopped tomatoes to the pan, along with the paprika, mixed herbs, chilli sauce and salt, and stir to combine. Bring the sauce to a gentle simmer and leave to cook for 5 minutes, then add the meatballs to the pan and turn the heat to low. Cook the meatballs in the sauce for 40 minutes, covered but stirring occasionally.

Once cooked, divide the meatballs and sauce between 4 serving plates and garnish with the fresh basil. Serve hot, with pasta or rice alongside.

Mr Singh's Fabulous Fiery Cookbook

CHORIZO AND EGGS IN TOMATO SAUCE

AMAR: My best friend Smita and I first came across this dish whilst holidaying in Spain. We were enjoying a few glasses of wine and the waiter brought over this incredible tapas dish which perfectly captured the sunny vibe we were enjoying. When I returned home, I invited Smita over for a catch up and decided to recreate the dish at home to transport us back to the wonderful weekend we had enjoyed together.

PREPARATION TIME: 15 MINUTES
COOKING TIME: 50 MINUTES

Serves 4

2 tbsp olive oil

200 g/7 oz chorizo,
    cut into 5 mm/¼ in slices

1 onion, finely chopped

2 garlic cloves, crushed

½ leek, finely diced

½ carrot, peeled and finely diced

½ red (bell) pepper, finely diced

1 tsp dried oregano

1 tsp paprika

½ tomato, finely chopped

2 tbsp Mr Singh's Hot Punjabi
    Chilli Sauce or Basic Chilli
    Sauce (see page 150)

1 x 400 g/14 oz tin chopped
    tomatoes

1 handful fresh basil, leaves torn

4 eggs

salt and freshly ground
    black pepper

fresh bread, to serve (optional)

Place the oil in a large ovenproof frying pan or skillet over a medium heat. Once hot, add the chorizo to the pan and cook, stirring occasionally, for 2 minutes, until starting to release their oil. Add the onion and garlic to the pan and continue to cook, stirring continuously, for 5 minutes, until the onions are soft and translucent.

Add the leek, carrot and red (bell) pepper to the pan and cook, stirring continuously, for another 5–7 minutes, until the vegetables are tender. Add the oregano and paprika to the pan and stir to combine.

Add the fresh tomatoes and chilli sauce to the pan and stir to combine, turn the heat to low and cook, stirring occasionally, for 5 minutes then add the chopped tomatoes to the pan along with 250 ml/9 fl oz/generous 1 cup of water and season to taste. Bring to a simmer and cook over a gentle heat for 40 minutes, until thick and unctuous, then stir in the basil.

Meanwhile, preheat the oven to 200°C/400°F/gas mark 6.

Crack the eggs on top of the tomato and chorizo mixture, placing one in each quarter of the pan. Transfer the pan to the oven and cook for 7–10 minutes, until the egg whites are cooked through but the yolks are still runny.

Divide the mixture between 4 serving plates, being careful not to break the egg yolks, and serve warm with fresh bread alongside for dipping.

ALOO PATHO

POPS: This vegetable curry is packed with flavour and can be on the table in half an hour, making it great for midweek meals. The chillies used in this dish pack a punch, so feel free to adjust the amount you use to suit your taste. This makes a delicious main course when served with rice or flatbreads, but would also make a great vegetable side dish for a big family feast.

PREPARATION TIME: 10 MINUTES

COOKING TIME: 30 MINUTES

Serves 4

2 tbsp olive oil

1 tsp cumin seeds

2 onions, thinly sliced

115 g/4 oz chopped tomatoes, blended until smooth

1 tsp salt

½ tsp garam masala

¼ tsp ground turmeric

4 green finger chillies, finely chopped

2 large potatoes, peeled and diced into 1 cm/¼ in cubes

8 baby aubergines (eggplants), slit down the middle

Cumin Rice (see page 126), to serve (optional)

chapatis, to serve (optional)

Place the oil in a large pan over a medium heat. Once hot, add the cumin seeds and onions and cook, stirring continuously, until the onions are soft and just starting to colour, around 5 minutes.

Add the tomatoes to the pan along with the salt, garam masala, turmeric and green chillies. Stir to combine and bring to a gentle simmer. Cook over a low heat until the oil starts to rise to the surface, around 2 minutes.

Add the potatoes and stir to coat in the sauce. Cook for 5 minutes, then add the aubergines (eggplants) to the pan and stir to combine. Place a lid on the pan and cook over a low heat, stirring occasionally, for around 15 minutes, until the potatoes and aubergines are tender.

Serve hot with Cumin Rice (see page 126) and chapatis alongside.

ALOO METHI

MAMA SINGH: It really is worth spending the time trying to find fresh fenugreek for this fragrant vegetable curry as its flavour is what brings this dish alive. This is the absolute favourite of my middle son, Rav, and he would happily exist on big steaming bowls of it – I hope that you enjoy it as much as he does!

PREPARATION TIME: 10 MINUTES

COOKING TIME: 55 MINUTES

Serves 4

5 tbsp vegetable or
   sunflower oil

1 tsp mustard seeds

6 garlic cloves, crushed

1 tsp salt

1 tsp ground turmeric

thumb-size piece fresh ginger,
   finely chopped

3 green finger chillies,
   finely chopped

2 bunches fresh fenugreek,
   finely chopped

200 g/7 oz chopped tomatoes,
   blended until smooth

4 potatoes, peeled and diced
   into 1 cm/½ in cubes

1 level tsp garam masala

salt and freshly ground pepper

plain yogurt, to serve (optional)

Handkerchief Roti (see page
   142), to serve (optional)

Place the oil in a large non-stick frying pan or skillet and heat over a medium flame. Once hot, add the mustard seeds and cook until they start to pop in the pan, about 1 minute. Turn the heat to low and add the garlic to the pan. Cook for 1 minute until the garlic starts to turn golden, being careful not to burn it, then quickly add the turmeric, ginger and chillies to the pan and cook for 5 minutes more, stirring continuously.

Add the chopped fenugreek to the pan and stir to coat in the spices, cook over a low heat for 30 minutes, stirring occasionally to stop it sticking to the bottom of the pan. After 30 minutes the fenugreek should look dark green and somewhat shrivelled in appearance (don't worry, it's not burnt!).

Add the tomatoes to the pan, season with salt and pepper and stir to combine. Cook for 1 minute, then add the potatoes to the pan and mix well. Place the lid on the pan and cook for 20 minutes, stirring occasionally, until the potatoes are tender.

Stir in the garam masala, being careful not to break up the potatoes. Serve warm with plain yogurt and Handkerchief Roti alongside.

RAJMA

SONIA: This protein-packed kidney bean curry takes me straight back to my youth. My mum used to use a pressure cooker to make this and hearing the whistle going off used to catch us unaware, but the finished product was so tasty that we learnt to associate the noise with the arrival of great food!

PREPARATION TIME: 15 MINUTES
COOKING TIME: 50 MINUTES

Serves 4

2½ tbsp olive oil

1 tsp cumin seeds

2 onions, finely chopped

100 g/3½ oz chopped tomatoes, blended until smooth

½ tbsp garlic and ginger paste

5 green finger chillies, finely chopped

1¼ tsp salt

½ tsp garam masala

¼ tsp ground turmeric

1 x 400 g/14 oz tin red kidney beans

1 medium potato, peeled and diced into 1 cm/½ in cubes

rice and chapatis, to serve (optional)

Heat the oil in a large pan over a medium heat. Once hot, add the cumin seeds and onions and cook, stirring continuously, until soft and golden brown, about 15 minutes.

Add the tomatoes, garlic and ginger paste, chillies, salt, garam masala and turmeric to the pan and stir to combine. Bring to a simmer, reduce the heat to low and cook for around 15 minutes, until the oil starts to pool on top of the tomatoes.

Pour the contents of the kidney bean tin, including the water, into the mixture and stir to combine. Add the potatoes along with 600 ml/20 fl oz/2½ cups boiling water and stir through.

Bring to a simmer then cook the mixture until the potatoes are tender and the liquid has thickened to a gravy consistency, around 20 minutes. If the curry is getting too thick, add a dash more water to the pan and place a lid on for the remainder of the cooking time.

Ladle the mixture into serving bowls and serve hot, either as it is or with rice and chapatis alongside for a more substantial meal.

CHOLE WITH PUFFED BREAD

POPS: When we first came to the UK, buying meat was a luxury and most of the dishes we prepared were vegetarian. This chickpea (garbanzo bean) curry is packed with protein and is a dish that benefits from simply sitting and simmering. We can eat as much meat as we like these days, but this is still one of my favourites.

PREPARATION TIME: 15 MINUTES

COOKING TIME: 45 MINUTES

Serves 4

2½ tbsp olive oil

1 tsp cumin seeds

2 onions, finely chopped

100 g/3½ oz tinned chopped tomatoes, blended smooth

½ tbsp garlic and ginger paste

5 green finger chillies, finely chopped

1¼ tsp salt

½ tsp garam masala

¼ tsp ground turmeric

1 x 400 g/14 oz tin chickpeas (garbanzo beans)

1 medium potato, diced

1 teabag

FOR THE PUFFED BREAD:

200 g/7 oz/generous 1½ cups self-raising (self-rising) flour

2 tbsp natural yogurt

2 tsp ajwain seeds

1 tsp salt

a dash of milk (if needed)

700 ml/1¼ pints/scant 2 cups vegetable oil

To make the chole, place the oil in a medium pan over a high heat. Once hot, add the cumin seeds and onions and cook, stirring continuously, for around 10 minutes, until the onions are golden. Add the tomatoes, garlic and ginger paste, chillies, salt, garam masala and turmeric to the pan and stir to combine. Bring the mixture to a simmer then turn the heat to low and cook, stirring occasionally, until the oil starts to rise to the surface, about 5 minutes.

Open the can of chickpeas (garbanzo beans) and pour the contents, including the water, into the pan along with the potatoes, the teabag and 600 ml/20 fl oz/2½ cups boiling water. Stir the mixture to combine then bring to a simmer and leave to cook over a medium heat for 10 minutes. Remove the teabag from the pan and discard. Give the mixture a stir and cover the pan with a lid. Leave the mixture to cook again for another 10 minutes or until the potatoes are tender and the sauce is nicely thickened.

While the chole is cooking, make the puffed flour breads. Place the flour, yogurt ajwain seeds and salt in a large bowl and bring together with your hands into a soft dough, adding a splash of milk if necessary. Set aside to rest for 15 minutes.

Meanwhile, place the oil in a large frying pan or skillet and heat to 180°C/350°F, or until a piece of dough immediately rises to the surface and fries to a golden brown.

Dust your work surface with flour and turn your rested dough out on to it. Divide the dough into 8 equal-size balls. Use a rolling pin to roll the balls into 13 cm/5 in rounds.

Working with one at a time, carefully lay the breads in the hot oil. Immediately start to press and stroke the surface of the bread with the back of slotted spoon or spatula – this encourages the breads to puff up while cooking. Once the bread has puffed up, flip it and cook on the reverse side until golden. Set aside while you cook the remainder.

Serve the chole warm with the breads alongside for scooping.

Mr Singh's Fabulous Fiery Cookbook

EGG PURJEE

SONIA: These are a kind of Indian scrambled egg, though that doesn't really do them justice as they are a far stretch away from the bland nursery food that most people associate with that description. They are packed with spices and bulked out with peas and tomatoes, so make a great quick lunch or lazy weekend brunch. You can serve these on toast, in a wrap, with chapatis or even in a toasted sandwich.

PREPARATION TIME: 5 MINUTES
COOKING TIME: 20 MINUTES

Serves 4

8 eggs

3 tbsp milk

4 tbsp sunflower or vegetable oil

2 onions, finely chopped

100 g/3½ oz chopped tomatoes, blended until smooth

3 green bird's-eye chillies, finely chopped (or to taste)

1 tsp salt

¼ tsp ground turmeric

70 g/2½ oz/½ cup frozen peas

1 tsp garam masala

1 handful fresh coriander (cilantro), finely chopped

Crack the eggs into a large mixing bowl and whisk until well combined, then add the milk and whisk again. Set aside.

Place the oil in a large pan over a medium heat. Once hot, add the onions to pan and cook, stirring constantly, until soft and golden brown, around 10 minutes. Add the tomatoes and chillies to the pan and cook, stirring, for 1 minute, then add the salt and turmeric and cook for 30 seconds more. Add the peas the pan and stir to combine, cook for 3 minutes, stirring constantly.

Pour the egg and milk mixture into the pan and cook, stirring constantly, for another 4 minutes, until the eggs are scrambled to your liking. Remove from the heat and stir in the garam masala and fresh coriander (cilantro).

Serve warm either on toast, in a wrap or in a toasted sandwich.

Mr Singh's Fabulous Fiery Cookbook

KENYAN SANDWICH

MAMA SINGH: My brothers, sister and I loved these sandwiches as children, our mum used to make them on rainy monsoon days. Eating these, my taste buds still tickle and I am transported straight back to my childhood with the smell of wet earth and the feeling of the rain dripping down the back of my neck.

PREPARATION TIME: 10 MINUTES

COOKING TIME: 35 MINUTES

Makes 4

3 tbsp vegetable or sunflower oil

¼ tsp black mustard seeds

2 garlic cloves, crushed

200 g/7 oz chopped tomatoes, blended until smooth

1 green bird's-eye chilli, finely chopped

1 tsp salt

½ tsp ground turmeric

2 carrots, peeled and finely chopped

1 large or 2 medium potatoes, peeled and diced into 1 cm/½ in cubes

70 g/2½ oz/½ cup frozen peas

½ tsp garam masala

1 handful fresh coriander (cilantro), chopped

8 slices of bread

butter, for spreading

To make the sandwich filling, place the oil in a large non-stick frying pan or skillet and heat over a medium flame. Once hot, add the mustard seeds and cook until they start to pop in the pan, about 1 minute. Turn the heat to low and add the garlic to the pan. Cook for 1 minute until the garlic starts to turn golden, being careful not to burn it, then stir in the tomatoes. Turn the heat to low and bring to a gentle simmer, then cook, covered, for 10 minutes, stirring occasionally.

Add the chilli, salt and turmeric to the pan and stir to combine. Cook for 5 minutes more, then add the chopped carrots to the pan and cook, covered, for a further 10 minutes, stirring occasionally.

Add the potatoes to the pan and stir to coat in the sauce. Cook, covered, for another 5 minutes, then add the peas to the pan to the pan and cook for 5 minutes more.

Remove the lid from the pan and cook for a final 10 minutes, until the potatoes are tender, then stir the garam masala into the mixture and scatter over the coriander (cilantro).

To assemble the sandwiches, toast the bread and spread with butter. Place a generous spoonful of the sandwich filling in the centre of a piece of toast and top with another. Repeat with the remaining sandwiches. Slice the sandwiches across the middle and serve warm.

GREEN GARLIC SOUP

MAMA SINGH: This soup has been in the Singh family for decades, though I only came across it after I married into the family. My mother-in-law used to prepare it when she was strapped for time and needed a quick meal, but it's full of deliciously fresh flavours and very nutritious.

PREPARATION TIME: 10 MINUTES

COOKING TIME: 30 MINUTES

Serves 4

450 g/1 lb garlic scapes (can be bought in Indian supermarkets)

1 medium onion, roughly chopped

115 g/4 oz unsalted butter

2 medium potatoes, peeled and diced into 1 cm/½ in cubes

1 tsp Mr Singh's Hot Punjabi Chilli Sauce or Basic Chilli Sauce (see page 150)

1 tsp garam masala

1 handful fresh coriander (cilantro), chopped, to garnish

To prepare the garlic scapes, trim away the root ends and peel away any tough outer leaves. Cut away the tough upper portion of the green leaves, then clean the remaining scapes under cold running water.

Chop the scapes into 2.5 cm/1 in pieces and place in a blender with 2 tablespoons of water. Pulse to a thin paste then transfer to a small bowl then set aside.

Place the onion in the blender and pulse to a smooth paste. Set aside.

Place the butter in a large pan over a medium heat and cook until melted. Add the pureed onion and cook, stirring occasionally, until translucent and tender. Add the garlic scape puree and potatoes to the pan and season with salt and pepper. Cook the mixture for 5 minutes, stirring continuously, then pour in 1.4 litres/ 2½ pints/ scant 6 cups of boiling water. Bring the mixture to the boil, then reduce to a simmer and cook for around 20 minutes, until the potatoes are tender.

Check the seasoning and ladle the soup into serving bowls and garnish with coriander (cilantro). Serve warm.

PUNJABI COLESLAW

AMAR: I've playfully called this 'coleslaw' as it contains the same core ingredients: crunchy cabbage and carrot. But here the ingredients are cooked till al dente in a spicy sauce. This is delicious on its own or as a side dish.

PREPARATION TIME: 5 MINUTES
COOKING TIME: 30 MINUTES

Serves 4

2 tbsp olive oil

1 tsp mustard seeds

4 garlic cloves, crushed

100 g/3½ oz tinned chopped tomatoes, blended until smooth

2 green finger chillies, finely chopped

1 tsp salt

½ tsp ground turmeric

½ tsp garam masala

1 small white cabbage, finely shredded

1 carrot, peeled and grated

1 handful fresh coriander (cilantro), finely chopped

Heat the oil in a large pan over a medium heat. Once hot, add the mustard seeds and cook, stirring continuously, until they start to pop, about 1 minute. Add the garlic to the pan and cook for 2 minutes, stirring continuously to ensure it doesn't burn.

Pour the blended chopped tomatoes into the pan and stir to combine with the spices. Bring to a gentle simmer then turn the heat to low and cook, stirring occasionally, for 5 minutes.

Add the chillies, salt, and turmeric to the pan and stir to combine. Leave to cook for 5 minutes so that the spices infuse with the sauce. Add the carrots and cook, covered, for 5 minutes more.

Add the cabbage to the pan and stir to coat in the sauce. Bring to a simmer and cook, covered, but stirring occasionally, for 10 minutes, until the cabbage is just tender but still retaining some bite.

Remove from the heat and stir in the garam masala and fresh coriander (cilantro.) Transfer to a serving bowl and serve warm.

KALE FRIED RICE

AMAR: Baked, steamed or stir-fried, kale adds flavour, colour and texture to any dish, not to mention being packed with nutrients. Kuldip and I have inspired moments where we go to local food markets and find unfamiliar vegetables to cook with. This is a result of discovering kale. We love it and hope that you do too.

PREPARATION TIME: 10 MINUTES
COOKING TIME: 10 MINUTES

Serves 4

400 g/14 oz/2 cups brown rice or 600 g/1 lb 5 oz/3 cups leftover cooked brown rice

1½ tbsp vegetable oil

2 eggs, beaten

1 tsp ground cumin

3 garlic cloves, crushed

2 tsp soy sauce

2 tsp chilli sauce

1 tbsp honey

1 tbsp balsamic vinegar

2 spring onions (scallions), finely sliced

½ red (bell) pepper, finely sliced

1 carrot, cut into fine batons

1 courgette (zucchini), cut into fine batons

thumb-size piece fresh ginger, finely chopped

150 g/5½ oz/scant 2 cups chopped kale

½ tsp pink Himalayan salt

juice of 1 lime

1 handful fresh coriander (cilantro), to garnish

If using fresh rice, cook according to pack instructions, rinse in boiling water and then set aside to cool.

Heat 1 tablespoon of the oil in a large wok over a high heat. Once hot, pour the beaten eggs into the wok and cook, stirring continuously, until scrambled. Transfer to a small bowl and set aside.

Return the wok to the heat with another half tablespoon of the oil, add the cumin to the pan and cook, stirring, for 1 minute, until fragrant. Add the garlic to the pan and cook, stirring to ensure that it doesn't burn, for 30 seconds, then add the soy sauce, chilli sauce, honey and balsamic vinegar and stir to combine.

Now add the spring onions (scallions), (bell) pepper, carrot, courgette (zucchini) and ginger to the pan and stir to coat in the sauce. Stir-fry the vegetables for 2 minutes, until tender but still retaining a bit of bite, then add the kale and salt and cook for 2 minutes more.

Now add the cooked rice and eggs back into the pan, breaking the rice up with a spatula, and stir-fry for 3 minutes, until hot and well combined. Pour over the lime juice and mix through the rice and vegetables.

Transfer the stir-fry to plates and serve hot, garnished with fresh coriander (cilantro).

BEETROOT, FETA AND CHILLI SALAD 🔥🔥

AMAR: This vibrant salad is packed with punchy flavours and can be thrown together in a matter of minutes, making it perfect for prepping ahead and enjoying *al-desko* at work or to serve as a side at a picnic or barbecue. Bird's-eye chillies may be small but they can be very potent, so feel free to add as much or as little as you like.

PREPARATION TIME: 5 MINUTES
COOKING TIME: N/A

Serves 4

150 g/5½ oz cooked beetroot (beets), coarsely grated

85 g/3 oz feta cheese, crumbled

2 small carrots, coarsely grated

½ onion, coarsely grated

juice of ½ lemon

1 tbsp olive oil

1 tbsp balsamic vinegar

1 large handful spinach

1 red bird's-eye chilli, finely chopped (or to taste)

salt and freshly ground pepper

Place the beetroot (beets), feta cheese, carrots and onion in a large bowl and mix to combine. In a small bowl, whisk together the lemon juice, olive oil and balsamic vinegar, then pour over the beetroot mixture.

Add the spinach to the bowl along with as much or as little of the chilli as you would like, then give everyting a good mix to ensure that everything is evenly distributed and well dressed.

Season to taste and serve.

MAIN MEALS

BAKED 'FRIED' CHICKEN

RAV: I love fried chicken but, like most people, I know it's really bad for me. This is my own version of the famous American fried chicken, but baked in the oven for a healthier end result. Don't worry though, it's still as deliciously moist inside and crunchy outside as any deep-fried version.

PREPARATION TIME: 10 MINUTES
COOKING TIME: 45 MINUTES

Serves 4

oil, for greasing
2 tbsp dried oregano
3 tsp salt
5 tsp ground black pepper
2 tsp garlic salt
2 tbsp dried basil
1 tbsp chilli powder (or more to taste)
1 tbsp paprika
60 g/2¼ oz/½ cup plain (all-purpose) flour
4 slices bread
5 eggs, beaten
4 chicken legs and thighs, skin on, lightly scored

Preheat the oven to 200°c/400°F/gas mark 6. Line a large baking sheet with foil and brush with oil to grease.

Place the bread into a food processor and pulse to form fine crumbs. Set aside.

Place three large bowls next to each other on the kitchen counter. Sift the flour into the first bowl, place the beaten eggs in the second and the breadcrumbs in the third.

Put all of the dried herbs and spices into another bowl, mixing to ensure they are well combined. Pour a quarter of the spice mixture into the bowl with the flour and mix to combine, then pour the remainder of the spices into the bowl with the breadcrumbs and mix to combine.

Now it's time to get your hands dirty! Take a piece of chicken and place in the bowl with the flour, turning it to ensure it is well coated. Now dip the chicken in the egg, again turning to ensure it is coated. Finally, place the chicken in the bowl with the breadcrumbs, rolling it to create an even crust all the way round. Place the chicken on the baking tray and repeat with the remaining chicken pieces.

Once you have completed coating all of your chicken pieces, ensure that they are evenly spaced on the baking sheet and transfer to the oven to cook for 25 minutes. After 25 minutes, remove the baking tray from the oven and carefully turn each piece of chicken over – use a spatula for this as the crumb can get stuck to the baking tray and fall off if it is not handled carefully. Return to the oven to cook for another 20 minutes until golden brown.

Serve hot with a big bowl of chilli sauce for dipping.

Mr Singh's Fabulous Fiery Cookbook

CLASSIC CHICKEN AND RICE

MAMA SINGH: Whether you are using our sauce or making your own from scratch, this is such a brilliant family dinner and is always at the centre of our informal family gatherings. It's quick and easy to prepare but also incredibly tasty – so maximum reward for minimum effort! Put a big bowl of this in the middle of the table and let everyone dive in!

PREPARATION TIME: 5 MINUTES
COOKING TIME: 30 MINUTES

Serves 4 –6

2 jars Mr Singh's Punjabi Pesto
or 1 quantity Thurka (see
page 152)

1 kg/2 lb 4 oz chicken breast,
cut into bite-sized pieces

1 handful fresh coriander
(cilantro)

Cumin Rice (see page 126),
to serve

naan bread or chapatis, to
serve (optional)

Place the Mr Singh's Punjabi Pesto or prepared Thurka in a large pan over a medium flame and heat to a gentle simmer. Add the chicken to the pan and cook for 10 minutes, until the chicken has turned white.

Add 1 litre/1¾ pints/generous 4 cups of boiling water to the pan and stir to combine, bring back to a simmer and leave to cook, uncovered, for 15 minutes more.

Serve the curry hot, garnished with fresh coriander (cilantro) and with Cumin Rice and your choice of breads alongside

SPINACH CHICKEN

MAMA SINGH: Like the recipe on the previous page, this is a real family favourite and a great dish for family dinners and celebrations. This one takes a bit more preparation, but is totally worth the effort and the extra cooking means that it gets elevated to slightly more 'special' occasions, in our house at least.

PREPARATION TIME: 10 MINUTES

COOKING TIME: 1 HOUR

Serves 4

2 tbsp olive oil

1 tsp cumin seeds

2 onions, finely chopped

2 garlic cloves, finely chopped

1 tsp ginger paste

225 g/9 oz tinned chopped tomatoes, blended until smooth

2 tsp salt

1 tsp garam masala

½ tsp ground turmeric

1 tsp chilli powder

200 g/7 oz fresh spinach, coarsely chopped

700 g/1 lb 9 oz chicken breast, cut into bite-size pieces

Cumin (see page 126) or Plain Rice (see page 128), to serve

chapatis, to serve

Place the oil in large frying pan or skillet over a medium heat. Once hot, add the cumin seeds and fry for 1 minute until fragrant. Add the onions and cook, stirring continuously, for about 10 minutes, until golden.

Add the garlic, ginger, tomatoes, salt, garam masala, turmeric and chilli powder to the pan with 4 tablespoons of cold water and stir to combine. Bring the mixture to a simmer and cook over a medium heat, stirring regularly, for 15 minutes, adding more water if the mixture starts to stick to the pan. Add the spinach to the pan and stir to combine then cook, stirring occasionally, for 10 minutes more.

Add the chicken to the pan and stir to combine. Cook for 10 minutes, stirring regularly, then pour in 850 ml/1½ pints/3½ cups boiling water and stir again. Leave to bubble away until the chicken is cooked through and the sauce has thickened to a gravy consistency.

Divide the mixture between 4 serving plates and serve hot with Cumin or Plain Rice and chapatis alongside.

LEFTOVER PIE

KULDIP: This was a dish that I first cobbled together one Boxing Day with the leftovers from Christmas dinner. It was such a hit that my wife, Amar, claimed it as her own and now tells everyone that she came up with it! Not just for Christmas time, this is a great one to pull out of the bag whenever you have leftover meat and veg in the house.

PREPARATION TIME: 10 MINUTES
COOKING TIME: 1 HOUR

Serves 4

4 tablespoons olive oil

½ bunch fresh thyme leaves

1 onion, finely chopped

3 garlic cloves, crushed

2 medium potatoes, peeled and diced into 1 cm/½ in cubes

2 leeks, chopped into chunks

300 g/10½ oz/2 cup leftover cooked vegetables, chopped into bite-size chunks

800 g/1 lb 12 oz leftover cooked meats, shredded

1 jar Mr Singh's Punjabi Pesto or ½ quantity Thurka (see page 152)

1.2 litres/2 pints/5 cups chicken or vegetable stock

2 tbsp Mr Singh's Hot Punjabi Chilli Sauce or Basic Chilli Sauce (see page 150)

500 g/1 lb 2 oz puff pastry

1 egg, beaten

plain (all-purpose) flour, for dusting

salt and freshly ground black pepper

Preheat the oven to 220°C/425°F/gas mark 7.

Place the oil in a large pan over a medium heat. Once hot, add the thyme, onions and garlic and cook, stirring continuously, until the onions are soft and golden, around 10 minutes.

Add the leeks to the pan and continue to cook for 5 minutes, stirring, until the leeks start to soften, then add the potatoes and cook for 5 minutes more. Stir in the leftover vegetables and meat and set aside.

In a separate pan, place the Punjabi Pesto or Thurka and chicken or vegetable stock over a medium heat. Stir to combine, then season with salt, pepper and chilli sauce as needed. Bring the mixture to a simmer then pour the sauce into the pan with the meat and vegetables, stirring to ensure that everything is well coated in the sauce. Transfer the mixture to a large ovenproof baking dish.

Flour your work surface then roll out the pastry to slightly larger than the size of your baking dish. Brush the edges of the baking dish with beaten egg then lay the pastry over the top, crimping at the edges to seal and trimming off any excess pastry. Brush the top of the pie with beaten egg and cut 2 small holes in the centre of the pastry lid to allow hot air to escape.

Transfer the pie to the oven and cook for 30–40 minutes, until the pastry lid is golden and well risen. Serve hot.

SPAM AND PUNJABI PESTO

SONIA: For some reason there is a bit of stigma attached to Spam, but it's cheap, tasty and great for store-cupboard dinners when the local supermarket just seems too far away. This is a dish my mum used to make us as children and is still a firm favourite with us all today.

PREPARATION TIME: 5 MINUTES
COOKING TIME: 35 MINUTES

Serves 4

½ tbsp olive oil

½ tsp cumin seeds

1 onion, finely sliced

100 g/3½ oz/scant ¾ cup frozen peas

150 g/5½ oz/scant 1 cup frozen sweetcorn

1 tbsp tomato puree

3 green finger chillies, finely chopped

½ tsp salt

¼ tsp garam masala

¼ tsp ground turmeric

1 tbsp Mr Singh's Hot Punjabi Chilli Sauce or Basic Chilli Sauce (see page 151)

1 x 340 g/12 oz tin Spam, diced into 1 cm/½ in cubes

chapatis, to serve

Place the oil in large pan over a medium heat. Once hot, add the cumin seeds and cook for 1 minute, stirring continuously, until fragrant. Add the onions to the pan and continue to cook, stirring, for 10 minutes, until soft and golden. Add the peas and sweetcorn to the pan and cook for 1 minute more.

Add the tomato puree, chillies, salt, garam masala and turmeric to the pan and stir to combine. Cook for 5 minutes, stirring occasionally, to allow the spices to infuse and become fragrant. Add the chilli sauce and spam to the pan and stir to coat in the sauce. Turn the heat to low, cover the pan and leave to cook for 15 minutes, stirring occasionally.

Divide the mixture between 4 serving plates and serve with chapatis alongside.

SPICY HAM FRITTATA

SONIA: This makes a perfect substantial lunch for those days when a sandwich just won't do. I like mine slathered in chilli sauce (ours obviously!), but you can tweak toppings and seasoning to make it your own.

PREPARATION TIME: 10 MINUTES
COOKING TIME: 20 MINUTES

Serves 4

8 eggs
½ tsp chilli powder
3 tsp salt
½ tsp pepper
½ tbsp olive oil
1 onion, finely chopped
½ red (bell) pepper, diced
100 g/3½ oz cooked ham or
  chicken, chopped
1 tsp mixed Italian herbs
1 tbsp chilli sauce, to serve
  (optional)

Preheat the grill (broiler) to high.

Crack the eggs into a large mixing bowl then add the chilli powder, salt and pepper and whisk until well combined. Set aside.

Place the oil in a large ovenproof frying pan or skillet over a medium heat, then add the onions and cook for 3 minutes, stirring continuously, until soft but not browned. Add the (bell) pepper to the pan and continue to cook for a further 5 minutes.

Pour the egg mixture into the pan and cook for 3 minutes more, then scatter the ham or chicken over the top of the frittata followed by the Italian herbs. Transfer the pan to underneath the preheated grill and cook for about 4 minutes, until puffed up and golden.

Using a spatula, carefully transfer the frittata on to a serving plate and slice into 4 portions. Serve hot, drizzled in chilli sauce and with salad alongside.

SINGH-STYLE PULLED PORK

KULDIP: I used to play American Football with a North London team. To watch big games, we would get together and devour platefuls of hot wings (see page 42) and this delicious pulled pork. The trick here is to cook the meat low and slow until unctuous and falling apart. Here, we've served the pork in chapatis to give it a Mr Singh's twist, but it works just as well in brioche bread rolls.

PREPARATION TIME: 6½ HOURS
COOKING TIME: 45 MINUTES

FOR THE RUB:

2½ tbsp dark muscavado sugar

2 tbsp garlic powder

2 tbsp dried mixed herbs

1½ tbsp chilli powder

2 tbsp fine sea salt

1½ tbsp freshly ground
   black pepper

FOR THE MEAT AND SAUCE:

1.8 kg/4 lbs shoulder of pork,
   neck end, bone in

1 knob butter

130 ml/4 fl oz/generous ½ cup
   Mr Singh's Punjabi chilli
   sauce or Basic Chilli Sauce
   (see page 150)

130 ml/4 fl oz/generous ½ cup
   Mr Singh's Punjabi Pesto or
   Thurka (see page 152)

5 tbsp Balsamic vinegar

Preheat your oven to 220°C/400°F/gas mark 7. Line a large roasting tin with foil, leaving a large flap to one side that can be used to cover the meat during cooking. Place your meat in the tin and set aside to come up to room temperature.

To make the rub, combine all of the ingredients in a bowl and mix to combine. Set 2 tablespoons of the mixture aside to use later and pour the rest over the meat. Using your hands, rub the spice mixture into the pork, ensuring that it is well coated on all sides. Transfer the meat to the oven, but do not cover it with the foil at this point. Cook for 30 minutes until the rub has started to form a crust and the pork skin is turning golden. Remove the meat from the oven and immediately turn the heat down to 130°C/250°F/gas mark ¼.

Add 4 tablespoons of water to the roasting pan and cover the meat with the foil flap, sealing the sides so steam can't escape. Return the meat to the oven and leave to cook at the lower temperature for 6 hours. Once cooked, remove the meat from the oven and set aside to rest, covered, for 20–30 minutes.

Once the meat has rested, drain any juices from the pan into a small bowl and set aside for use in the sauce. Then, using 2 forks, 'pull' the pork into thin strips – the meat should be deliciously soft and fall apart easily. Sprinkle the spice rub that you saved earlier over the meat and mix to combine. Cover with foil and set aside.

To make the sauce, melt the butter in a medium pan over low heat, then pour in the chilli sauce, Punjabi pesto or Thurka and balsamic vinegar. Add the reserved meat juices and stir to combine. Warm over a gentle heat for 5–10 minutes until the mixture starts to thicken.

Serve the pork warm inside a chapatti or soft bread roll with the sauce spooned over and coleslaw on the side.

Mr Singh's Fabulous Fiery Cookbook

SPICY GARLIC AND GINGER RIBS

RAV: This recipe came from my love of Chinese spare ribs and watching *Man Vs Food*. I don't have a pit smoker, BBQ or anything like that in my flat, but I WANTED RIBS! So I figured the 'low and slow' idea of barbecuing would also work in the the oven and, after a few attempts, it did!

PREPARATION TIME: 1½ HOURS
COOKING TIME: 4 HOURS

Serves 4

½ rack baby back pork ribs

FOR THE SAUCE:

1 bottle Mr Singh's BBQ Chilli Sauce or 1 quantity basic sweet chilli sauce (see page 151)
8 tbsp honey
5 tbsp garlic paste
5 tbsp ginger paste

FOR THE RUB:

6 tbsp garlic salt
3 tbsp salt
6 tbsp freshly ground pepper
5 tbsp chilli powder
6 tbsp everyday seasoning

Preheat the oven to 200°C/400°F/gas mark 6 and take your ribs out of the fridge to come up to room temperature. Line a large roasting pan with foil, leaving a large flap to one side that can be used to cover the ribs whilst they are cooking.

To make the dry rub, place all of the ingredients in a bowl, stir to combine and set aside.

Place the ribs in the prepared roasting pan and coat with 2–3 handfuls of the rub. Set the remaining dry rub aside to be used later in the sauce. Cover the ribs with the foil and seal at the edges to completely enclose. Transfer to the oven to cook for 30 minutes.

Meanwhile, make the sauce by placing the chilli sauce in a bowl with the honey, ginger and garlic pastes and the remaining dry rub mixture and stir to combine. Set aside.

After the ribs have been cooking for 30 minutes, remove them from the oven and carefully peel back the foil. Using a basting or pastry brush, generously slather the ribs with some of the sauce, making sure they are well coated. Loosely cover the ribs with the foil again and return to the oven. Repeat this process every half an hour, until the ribs have been cooking for a total of 4 hours.

After 4 hours, the ribs should be sticky and unctuous with the meat falling of the bones. Transfer to a serving platter and dig straight in with your hands.

LASAGNE WITH A KICK

SONIA: Believe it or not, there are times when even we don't fancy a curry. Lasagne is one of those dishes that every family has a version of and this is ours, with our signature Singh-style chilli kick. Lasagne purists will probably balk at the presence of ginger and chilli in this, but it really works and always has everyone smiling around our table.

PREPARATION TIME: 25 MINUTES

COOKING TIME: 1 HOUR
45 MINUTES

Serves 4

2 tbsp olive oil

1 kg/2 lb 4 oz minced (ground) lamb

2 onions, finely chopped

½ tbsp garlic and ginger paste

1 x 400 g/14 oz tin chopped tomatoes, blended until smooth

1½ tbsp tomato puree

3 green finger chillies, finely chopped

1 tbsp dried mixed Italian herbs

dried lasagne sheets

salt and freshly ground pepper

FOR THE CHEESE SAUCE:

50 g/1¾ oz butter

3 tbsp plain (all-purpose) flour

300 ml/½ pint/1¼ cups whole milk

50 g/1¾ oz Cheddar cheese, grated

Place the oil in a large pan over a medium heat. Once hot, add the minced (ground) lamb to the pan and break it up with a spatula or wooden spoon. Fry the meat, stirring continuously, until browned. Add the onions and garlic and ginger paste and continue to cook, stirring, until the onions are soft and translucent, about 5 minutes.

Add the tomatoes, tomato puree, chillies and herbs and stir to combine. Bring the mixture to a simmer then turn the heat to low and leave to cook, stirring occasionally for 30 minutes. Season to taste and set aside.

Preheat your oven to 200°C/400°F/gas mark 6.

To make the cheese sauce, melt the butter in a medium pan over a low heat. Once the butter has melted, tip the flour into the pan and whisk into the butter with a wooden spoon, cook for 2 minutes, stirring continuously, to allow the flavour of the flour to cook off. Add a third of the milk and whisk to incorporate into the flour mixture, once nicely thickened add another third of the milk and thicken again. Add the final third of the milk and whisk to incorporate, cook until thick enough to coat the back of a spoon then stir in three quarters of your grated cheese. Take the pan off the heat ready to assemble your lasagne.

To assemble the lasagne, spread half of the meat mixture in the base of a large baking dish and cover with lasagne sheets. Spread a layer of cheese sauce over the top of the lasagne sheets then repeat the layers again, finishing with a layer of cheese sauce.

Cover the baking dish with foil and transfer to the oven to cook for 45 minutes. Remove the lasagne from the oven, take off the foil and scatter over the remaining cheese. Return the lasagne to the oven and cook, uncovered, for 20 minutes, until golden and bubbling. Serve hot, with salad (or chips!!) alongside.

Mr Singh's Fabulous Fiery Cookbook

KEEMA AND PEAS

MAMA SINGH: This spicy curry made with minced (ground) lamb is a staple in many Indian households and each family will have their own special way of preparing it. My sons love this classic dish and always fight over the leftovers so that they can use it to make toasties the next day.

PREPARATION TIME: 5 MINUTES
COOKING TIME: 1 HOUR 10 MINUTES

Serves 4

3 tbsp sunflower or vegetable oil

5 onions, finely chopped

5 garlic cloves, crushed

1 x 400 g/14 oz tin chopped tomatoes, blended until smooth

thumb-size piece fresh ginger, finely chopped

4 green finger chillies, finely chopped

1 tsp salt

1 tsp ground turmeric

600 g/1 lb 5 oz minced (ground) lamb

70 g/2½ oz/½ cup frozen peas

1 tsp garam masala

1 handful fresh coriander (cilantro), finely chopped

Place the oil in a large pan over a medium heat. Once hot, add the onions and garlic and cook, stirring continuously, until the onions are soft and golden brown, around 20 minutes.

Add the tomatoes to the pan and stir to combine. Bring to simmer, turn the heat to low and cook, stirring occasionally, for 10 minutes. Add the ginger and chillies to the pan and continue to cook, still stirring, until the oil starts to pool on the surface of the tomatoes, around 5 minutes. Add the salt and turmeric to the pan, stir to combine and cook for 1 minute more.

Add the minced (ground) lamb to the pan and break up with a wooden spoon or spatula. Stir well to ensure the lamb is coated in the sauce then bring to a gentle simmer and cook, stirring occasionally, for 25 minutes, or until the lamb is cooked through. Add the peas to the pan and cook for a final 10 minutes. If the mixture is too dry add 100 ml/3½ fl oz/scant ½ cup boiling water along with the peas.

Stir in the garam masala and transfer the keema to serving plates. Garnish with fresh coriander (cilantro) and serve hot.

HOT AND SPICY LAMB CHOPS 🔥

RAV: I love lamb chops and they are my go-to item on any menu when I go out for dinner, the only problem being that the ones I make at home are always better! These are sweet, spicy and minty, making them a vibrant starting point for any meal on a summer's evening. These need to be marinated for at least 5 hours, but for best results ideally overnight.

PREPARATION TIME: 15 MINUTES, PLUS MARINATING

COOKING TIME: 10 MINUTES

Serves 4

4 lamb chops
salad and roasted vegetables, to serve (optional)

FOR THE MARINADE:

4 tbsp mint jelly
1 tbsp salt
3 tbsp freshly ground pepper
3 tbsp chilli powder
4 tbsp runny honey
3 tbsp garlic and ginger paste

Lay the lamb chops flat in the base of large baking dish and set aside.

To make the marinade, place all of the ingredients in a bowl and whisk to combine. Pour the marinade over the lamb and use your hands to ensure that everything is well coated. Cover the baking dish with cling film (plastic wrap) and transfer to the fridge for at least 5 hours, but ideally overnight.

Take the lamb chops out of the fridge 30 minutes before you want to cook them to allow them to come to room temperature. When ready to cook the lamb chops, place a large griddle pan over a high heat and leave for 10–15 minutes, until very hot and you see smoke rising from the pan.

Lay the chops on the hot pan and pour half of any residual marinade from the baking dish over the top. Cook for 3–5 minutes, then flip the chops and pour over the rest of the reserved marinade. Cook for another 3–5 minutes, depending on how pink you like your lamb, then remove from the heat and transfer to serving plates.

Serve the chops hot with salad and roasted vegetables for a great summery dinner.

KEEMA KOFTA

MAMA SINGH: Though I sometimes caved to my son's demands and made my twist on Italian-style meatballs (see page 66) when they were young, more often I made this classic Indian dish of spiced lamb kofta in a fragrant gravy. Another classic, this is a recipe that was taught to me by my own mother and now I am sharing with you.

PREPARATION TIME: 15 MINUTES
COOKING TIME: 50 MINUTES

Serves 4

600 g/1 lb 5 oz minced (ground) lamb

5 garlic cloves, crushed

3 green finger chillies, finely chopped

1 tsp salt

2 jars Mr Singh's Punjabi Pesto or 1 quantity Thurka (see page 152)

1 handful fresh coriander (cilantro), chopped, to garnish

Plain Rice (see page 128) and flatbreads, to serve

Place the minced (ground) lamb, garlic, chillies and salt in a large mixing bowl and mix everything together thoroughly with your hands. Divide the mixture into 16 equal pieces and roll each piece into a ball in the cupped palm of your hand. Set aside.

Place the Punjabi Pesto or Thurka in a large pan over a medium heat and bring to a simmer, turn the heat to low and leave to cook, stirring occasionally, for 10 minutes. Add the lamb balls to the pan and shake carefully to cover with the sauce.

Add 3 tablespoons of water to the pan, but do not stir into the sauce, then leave to cook over a low heat for 30 minutes, occasionally shaking the pan to ensure the lamb balls aren't sticking to the base.

Add 500 ml/18 fl oz/generous 2 cups boiling water to the pan and mix to combine. Cook for 10 minutes more to allow the sauce to thicken to a gravy consistency.

Garnish the kofta with fresh coriander (cilantro) and serve hot with Plain Rice and flatbreads alongside.

FRAGRANT LAMB CURRY

KULDIP: This warming lamb curry is perfect for battening down the hatches and curling up on the sofa on a lazy Sunday afternoon. Don't be put off by the amount of ingredients, they come together to create a marvellous depth of flavour. For added ease, this can be prepared in the slow cooker – simply follow the recipe until you have browned the lamb, then tip everything into the slow cooker and leave to bubble away until the meat is falling apart and deliciously tender.

PREPARATION TIME: 15 MINUTES
COOKING TIME: 1 HOUR

2 tbsp ghee or vegetable oil

2 onions, finely chopped

5 garlic cloves, crushed

thumb-size piece fresh ginger, peeled and grated

3 green cardamom pods, lightly crushed

1½ tsp cumin seeds, lightly crushed

2 cloves

1 cinnamon stick

1½ tsp ground coriander

1 tsp paprika

1 tsp ground turmeric

1½ tsp salt

3 green finger chillies (optional), chopped

600g/1lb 5 oz diced lamb leg

150ml/¼ pint/generous ½ cup double (heavy) cream

1 tbsp flaked almonds

1 handful fresh coriander (cilantro) leaves, to garnish

Cumin Rice (see page 126) and flatbreads, to serve

Place the ghee or vegetable oil in a large stockpot or flameproof casserole dish (Dutch oven) over a low flame, add the onions and garlic and cook, stirring continuously, until soft and just starting to turn golden, about 10 minutes. Add the ginger and continue to cook for 2 minutes more.

Add the cardamom pods, cumin, cloves, cinnamon stick, paprika, turmeric, salt and chillies to the pan and continue to cook, still stirring, for 4 minutes until fragrant.

Add the lamb to the pan and stir to coat in the spice and onion mix. Cook the lamb until browned then pour in 250 ml/9 fl oz/generous 1 cup boiling water and stir to combine. Bring the liquid to a boil, then reduce the heat to a simmer and leave to cook, covered, for 40 minutes until the lamb is tender.

Stir the cream into the pan and cook for a further 5 minutes, then stir in the flaked almonds. Serve hot with Cumin (see page 126) or Plain Rice (see page 128) and flatbreads alongside.

STUFFED PEPPERS

This is a great dish for a summer's evening. Though it looks light, the lamb and couscous stuffing is very filling, so don't be fooled by appearances. We've made these quite spicy but feel free to amend to your own tastes. If you're feeding vegetarians, omitting the lamb filling and doubling up the couscous would work well.

PREPARATION TIME: 25 MINUTES

COOKING TIME: 45 MINUTES

Serves 4

4 red or yellow (bell) peppers

100 g/3½ oz/scant 1 cup grated
   Cheddar cheese

FOR THE LAMB FILLING:

1 tbsp olive oil

500 g/1 lb 2 oz minced lamb

1 onion, finely chopped

½ tsp cumin seeds

115 g/4 oz chopped tomatoes,
   blended until smooth

½ tbsp tomato puree

4 green finger chillies, chopped

½ tbsp garlic and ginger paste

1 tsp dried mixed Italian herbs

FOR THE COUSCOUS:

½ tbsp olive oil

1 carrot, peeled and diced

50 g/1¾ oz/½ cup sweetcorn

1 tsp garlic powder

½ tsp salt

½ tsp paprika

200 g/7 oz/1 cup couscous

Preheat the oven to 190°C/375°F/gas mark 5.

To make the lamb filling, heat the oil in a large pan over a medium heat. Once hot add the lamb, breaking it up with a wooden spoon or spatula, and cook, stirring continuously, until browned. Add the onions and cumin seeds and continue to cook, stirring, until the onions are soft and translucent.

Add the tomatoes, tomato puree, chillies, garlic and ginger paste and dried herbs to the pan alond with 300 ml/½ pint/1½ cups of cold water and stir to combine. Bring the mixture to a gentle simmer and cook, stirring occasionally, until the liquid has reduced and thickened, about 25 minutes. Set aside.

Remove and discard the tops and central cores of the (bell) peppers. Place the peppers, top side up, on a baking sheet and roast in the oven for 30 minutes.

Meanwhile, make the couscous. Heat the oil in a large pan over a medium heat. Once hot, add the carrot, sweetcorn, garlic powder, salt and paprika and stir to combine. Reduce the heat to low and cook, stirring continuously, for about 10 minutes, until the carrots are tender.

Pour 300 ml/½ pint/1½ cups boiling water into the pan then pour in your couscous in one smooth movement. Stir the couscous once, then remove the pan from the heat and set aside, covered, for 10 minutes, until cooked. Once cooked, fluff up the couscous with a fork and set aside until your peppers are cooked.

Spoon the couscous into the base of the cooked peppers to half fill each one. Top with the lamb mixture and scatter over the grated cheese. Return the peppers to the oven and cook until the cheese is golden and bubbling, about 10 minutes.

Transfer to serving plates and serve the peppers hot with salad alongside.

Mr Singh's Fabulous Fiery Cookbook

TUNA FISHCAKES

SONIA: These fishcakes are a great make-ahead meal that can be on the table in just a few minutes, so are perfect for rushed midweek suppers. We've given these the Mr Singh's treatment and added some spice and fire to elevate them into something a bit special, but you can cut down (or ramp up!) the chilli to suit your taste.

PREPARATION TIME: 10 MINUTES, PLUS RESTING

COOKING TIME: 6 MINUTES

Serves 4

1 large potato, peeled and diced into 1 cm/½ in cubes

225 g/8 oz tinned tuna, drained and rinsed

¼ onion, finely chopped

1 egg, beaten

1 tsp garlic salt

1 tsp mixed herbs

¼ tsp cayenne pepper

1 tsp Mr Singh's Hot Punjabi Chilli Sauce or Basic Chilli Sauce (see page 150), plus extra for dipping

3 tbsp plain (all-purpose) flour

1 tbsp olive oil

salt and freshly ground pepper

mixed salad, to serve (optional)

Place the potato in a medium pan and pour over cold water to cover. Place over a high heat and bring to the boil, then lower the heat to a gentle simmer and leave to cook until tender, about 15 minutes. Drain the potatoes then return to the pan and mash until smooth. Set aside to cool.

Flake the tuna into a mixing bowl, then add the onion, egg, garlic salt, mixed herbs, cayenne pepper, chilli sauce and 2 tablespoons of the flour. Mix to combine and season to taste. Divide the mixture into 4 equal-size balls, then press each ball down to form a patty around 3 cm/1¼ in thick. Place the fishcakes on a plate, cover and transfer to the fridge for an hour to firm up.

Place the remaining tablespoon of flour on a small plate and press the fishcakes lightly into the flour to coat.

Heat the oil in large frying pan or skillet over a medium heat. Once hot, place the fishcakes in the pan and cook for 3 minutes on one side then flip over and cook for another 3 minutes. Serve hot with salad and extra chilli sauce alongside for drizzling.

SPICED FISH PARCELS

AMAR: This is an effortless way of cooking a tasty and nutritious meal that has the added bonuses of both looking sophisticated and creating barely any washing up! Kuldip and I first came across this method of cooking while watching a cooking show on TV and decided to give it a go ourselves. This also works just as well with other white flaky fish.

PREPARATION TIME: 10 MINUTES
COOKING TIME: 20 MINUTES

Serves 4

4 tsp butter

4 garlic cloves, crushed

4 skinless, boneless cod fillets, around 150 g/5½ oz each

chilli flakes, to taste

12 new potatoes, cut into 5 mm/¼ in slices

1 large carrot, finely chopped

250 g/9 oz/2 cups sugar snap peas

8 baby corn

150 g/5½ oz green beans

juice of 2 limes

salt and freshly ground black pepper

Preheat the oven to 180°C/350°F/gas mark 4 and cut 4 large squares of foil.

Place the butter and garlic in a small bowl and mix to combine. Set aside.

Lay your foil squares out side by side and place a fillet of cod in the centre of each. Top each fillet of fish with a teaspoon of the garlic butter, rubbing it into the flesh to ensure an even coating. Season the fish with salt, pepper and chilli flakes.

Lay the potato slices over the fish and scatter over the rest of the vegetables, season again. Pour a quarter of the lime juice over each pile of fish and vegetables, then bring up the edges of the foil and crimp together to make a sealed parcel, ensuring the there is enough space around the fish for steam to be created.

Place on a baking sheet and transfer to the oven to cook for 20 minutes. Once cooked, transfer the contents of each parcel to a serving plate and serve hot.

COD WITH PUNJABI PESTO

MAMA SINGH: When we first came to the UK we were amazed by the British obsession with fish and chips. Looking to add some spice, I decided to reinvent the fish, cooked in a spicy sauce rather than the traditional batter. Though we've now come to appreciate the charms of the local fish shop, this is still our go-to recipe at home.

PREPARATION TIME: 15 MINUTES
COOKING TIME: 20 MINUTES

Serves 4

4 skinless, boneless cod or haddock fillets, around 150 g/5½ oz each

1 jar Mr Singh's Punjabi Pesto or ½ quantity Thurka (see page 152)

5 tbsp lemon juice

½ tsp salt

1 handful fresh coriander (cilantro) leaves, to garnish

Triple-cooked Chips (see page 129), to serve

peas, to serve

Preheat the oven to 190°C/375°F/gas mark 5.

Place the fish fillets in a dish and sprinkle over 2 tablespoons of the lemon juice to evenly coat on both sides then sprinkle the salt over the top. Set aside for 10 minutes to absorb the flavour of the lemon.

Place the fish flat in the base of a large baking dish and pour over the Punjabi Pesto or Thurka, ensuring that all of the fish is well covered. Transfer to the oven and cook for 15–20 minutes, until the fish is cooked through and flaky.

Divide the fish fillets and sauce among 4 serving plates and drizzle over the remaining lemon juice. Garnish with fresh coriander (cilantro) and serve with Triple-cooked Chips and peas alongside.

BLACK CHICKPEA STEW

MAMA SINGH: Black chickpeas (garbanzo beans) are chewier and more filling than their white counterparts and have a nuttier flavour. You can buy them canned in good Indian supermarkets and dried in many health food stores. If using the dried variety, follow the pack instructions for soaking and cooking them and then follow the recipe as below.

PREPARATION TIME: 10 MINUTES
COOKING TIME: 45 MINUTES

Serves 4

2 jars Mr Singh's Punjabi Pesto or 1 quantity Thurka (see page 152)

2 x 400 g/14 oz cans black chickpeas (garbanzo beans), drained

2 medium potatoes, peeled and diced into 1 cm/½ in cubes

1 tsp garam masala

1 handful fresh coriander (cilantro) leaves, to garnish

Cumin Rice (see page 126) and flatbreads, to serve

Place the Punjabi Pesto or Thurka in a large pan over medium heat and bring to a simmer. Reduce the heat to low and leave to cook, stirring occasionally, for 10 minutes, until slightly thickened.

Reserve 4 tablespoons of the chickpeas to use later and pour the rest into the pan with the sauce, stirring to combine. Continue to cook, stirring occasionally, for 10 minutes, adding a splash of water to the pan if the mixture is too thick or starting to stick.

Place the reserved chickpeas into a blender and pulse to a smooth paste, adding a splash of water if necessary. Stir the chickpea paste into the pan with whole chickpeas and sauce.

Add the potatoes to the pan along with 1 litre/1¾ pints/generous 4 cups boiling water and stir to combine. Bring back to a simmer and cook for around 20 minutes, until the potatoes are tender and the sauce has thickened to a gravy consistency.

TOOR DHAL

POPS: Dhal is a staple dish in most Indian homes and it's not hard to see why: lentils are cheap, easy to prepare, packed with protein and make a great base for other flavours. This is a great dish to make if you're doing an Indian feast and have vegetarians coming for dinner, just be prepared to fight off the meat eaters!

PREPARATION TIME: 10 MINUTES

COOKING TIME: 1 HOUR

Serves 4

100 g/3½ oz/½ cup dried pink lentils (masoor dhal), rinsed

100 g/3½ oz/½ cup dried split mung beans (moong dhal), rinsed

1 tsp salt

¼ tsp ground turmeric

1 tbsp ghee (clarified butter)

2 green bird's-eye chillies, finely chopped

½ tsp cumin Seeds

1 tsp garam masala

1 onion, finely chopped

1 handful fresh coriander (cilantro) leaves, to garnish

Cumin Rice (see page 126) and flatbreads, to serve

Place the pink lentils and split mung beans together in a large pan with 1.5 litres/ 2½ pints/6¼ cups of water over a high heat. Bring to a boil then reduce the heat to a simmer and cook, covered and stirring occasionally, for 30 minutes. Add the salt and turmeric to the pan and cook for 15 minutes more.

Meanwhile, melt the ghee over a low heat in a small pan. Once melted, add the cumin seeds and cook, stirring, for 1 minute, until fragrant. Add the onions to the pan and cook, stirring continuously, until soft and golden brown, around 15 minutes.

Add the onion mixture to the dahl and stir to combine. Continue to cook, uncovered, until thick and soupy, around 20 minutes, then remove from the heat and stir in the garam masala.

Serve the dahl hot, garnished with fresh coriander (cilantro) and with rice and flatbreads alongside.

SIDE DISHES

CUMIN RICE

KULDIP: There is a tendency to regard rice simply as the vehicle to carry other components of a meal, but with a little care it can be a star in its own right. A big bowl of this rice is always in the centre of the table at any large Singh family gathering and it makes the perfect fragrant accompaniment to any of the curries in this book.

PREPARATION TIME: 5 MINUTES
COOKING TIME: 20 MINUTES

Serves 4

2 tbsp vegetable oil
1 tsp salt
1 tsp cumin seeds
185g/6½ oz/1 cup basmati rice, rinsed in 2 changes of water

Place the oil in a large pan over a medium heat, then add the cumin seeds and cook for about 1 minute until they start to pop and smell fragrant. Add the rice to the pan and stir to coat the grains in the oil. Pour over 480ml/16 fl oz/2 cups boiling water and stir once to combine.

Bring the rice to a boil then turn the heat down to a gentle simmer and stir in the salt. Cover the pan and cook for 15–20 minutes, stirring occasionally, until the water has been absorbed and the grains of rice are tender.

Transfer the rice to a serving dish, fluff up with a fork and serve hot.

PLAIN RICE

MAMA SINGH: Though it seems simple, rice is one of those dishes that people are always telling me that they struggle with. Without following the right technique, it's easy to end up with an unappetizing, gloopy mess. Below is a foolproof method for perfect rice every time.

PREPARATION TIME: 5 MINUTES
COOKING TIME: 15 MINUTES

Serves 4

200 g/7 oz/generous 1 cup
    basmati rice, thoroughly
    rinsed

1 tsp salt

1 tbsp vegetable oil

Place the rice in a large pan with 500 ml/18 fl oz/generous 2 cups boiling water. Bring to the boil then reduce to a gentle simmer.

Add the salt and vegetable oil to the pan and leave to cook over a gentle heat, covered, for 15 minutes. Remove the pan from the heat and stir the rice – it should be cooked, fluffy and ready to serve.

TRIPLE-COOKED CHIPS

BUTCH: One hungover Sunday we were sat craving a soggy bag of chips and obviously no one wanted to make the effort to get dressed and leave the house to fetch them. I decided to bite the bullet and make my own and the result was far superior to anything that you get wrapped in newspaper.

PREPARATION TIME: 15 MINUTES

COOKING TIME: 50 MINUTES

Serves 4

6 large potatoes, skin on, cut into wedges

3 tbsp olive oil

2 tsp salt

1½ tbsp pepper

2 tsp cayenne pepper, or to taste

1 tsp garlic salt

Mr Singh's Punjabi Chilli Sauce or Basic Chilli Sauce (see page 150)

Preheat the oven to 200°C/400°F/gas mark 6 and line a large baking sheet with foil.

Place the sliced potatoes in a colander and rinse under the cold tap for a few minutes to remove any starch. Drain and then dry on a clean kitchen towel.

Transfer the potatoes to a large bowl and pour over the olive oil, using your hands to mix them up and ensure they are well coated.

In a small bowl, combine the salt, pepper, cayenne and garlic salt and mix to ensure it is evenly distributed. Sprinkle this mixture over the chips and again mix with your hands to ensure the potatoes are evenly coated.

Lay the chips flat on your prepared baking sheet. Do not overcrowd them as they will not go crispy if you do. If you are running out of space use an additional baking sheet. Place in the oven for 50 minutes, turning the chips halfway through. Serve hot with chilli sauce alongside.

HIMALAYAN POTATOES

KULDIP: This moreish dish makes a great accompaniment to any meat or fish main course. The pesto gives a subtle heat to the crispy potato chunks and the balsamic vinegar adds a delicious tang. Unfortunately there isn't any substitute for the Mr Singh's Himalayan Pesto, so you will have to go out and buy some if you want to make this (shameless, us?).

PREPARATION TIME: 5 MINUTES
COOKING TIME: 50 MINUTES

Serves 4

750g/1lb 10oz white potatoes (we use maris pipers), peeled and cut into bite-sized chunks

2½ tbsp Mr Singh's Himalayan Pesto

1 tbsp balsamic vinegar

1 tbsp olive oil

salt and pepper, to season

Preheat the oven to 180°C/350°F/gas mark 4.

Place the potatoes in a large pan and pour over cold water to cover. Place over a high heat and bring to a boil, then reduce the heat to a simmer and cook for 8 minutes until softened but still holding their shape. Drain the potatoes through a colander and transfer to a large baking pan.

In a small bowl, combine the Himalaya pesto, balsamic vinegar and olive oil. Pour the mixture over the potatoes and move everything around to make sure it is well coated. Season the potatoes with salt and pepper and transfer to the oven for 40 minutes, giving them a mix halfway through the cooking time.

Remove from the oven, transfer to a serving dish and serve hot.

SPICY SWEET POTATO WEDGES ♨

BUTCH: Sweet potatoes are packed with the delicious starchy flavours that we all crave when we go hunting for chips, but are actually far better for us than regular potatoes. If I'm trying to be healthy or am just looking for something a little lighter, these are my go to 'chip'.

PREPARATION TIME: 25 MINUTES
COOKING TIME: 45 MINUTES

Serves 4

1.25 kg/2 lb 12 oz sweet
   potatoes, cut into wedges
1 litre/1¾ pints/generous
   4 cups vegetable or
   sunflower oil, for frying
1 tbsp chilli powder
1 tbsp Himalayan salt
lemon wedges, to serve

Place the sweet potato wedges in a large pan and pour over cold water to cover. Place the pan over a high heat and bring to a boil, then reduce to a simmer and cook the potatoes until just tender but still holding their shape, about 6 minutes. Drain the potatoes and lay out on a wire rack until cool. Once cooled, transfer the potatoes to the fridge for at least 30 minutes or until ready to use.

Meanwhile, heat the oil in a large wok or deep pan to 180°C/350°F, or until a piece of potato floats on the surface of the oil and cooks to a golden brown.

Once the oil is up to temperature, carefully place a third of the sweet potato wedges in the oil and leave to cook for 5–7 minutes, until crunchy and golden brown. Remove from the oil and leave to rest on a sheet of kitchen paper to drain of excess oil while you cook the remaining batches of potatoes.

In a small bowl, combine the chilli powder and salt then scatter the mixture over the wedges. Transfer to a serving bowl and serve hot, with lemon wedges alongside.

ONION RINGS

BUTCH: Onion rings are one of those essential sides that I always have to order at a burger or fast-food restaurant, so I had to try and make them myself at home. The thing I love most about them is the level of crunch that they bring to a meal, so I developed a system of double dipping in breadcrumbs to ensure they had maximum bite!

PREPARATION TIME: 15 MINUTES
COOKING TIME: 10 MINUTES

Serves 4

6 slices bread

1 large onion, cut into 5 mm/¼ in slices, rings separated

1 litre/1¾ pints/generous 4 cups vegetable or sunflower oil, for frying

2 eggs, beaten

125 g/4½ oz/1 cup plain (all-purpose) flour

2 tbsp salt

2 tbsp freshly ground pepper

3 tbsp five spice

Place the bread in a food processor and pulse to create fine breadcrumbs. Add the salt, pepper and five spice to the processor and pulse again to combined. Place the seasoned breadcrumbs in a large bowl and set aside until needed.

Prepare your work surface by lining up your bowls of flour, beaten eggs and seasoned breadcrumbs next to each other. The key to making these really crunchy is to 'double dip' the onion rings in the breadcrumbs. Working one at a time, take an onion ring and coat it in the flour, then dip immediately into the egg and then into the bread-crumbs to coat. Now return the coated rings to the egg and then finally back into the breadcrumbs to create a double coating. Place the coated rings on your baking sheet while you continue with the rest. Once all the rings are coated, transfer to the fridge to chill for at least 30 minutes before cooking.

Heat the oil in a large wok or deep pan to 180°C/350°F, or until a piece of onion floats on the surface of the oil and cooks to a golden brown. Line a large baking sheet with baking parchment.

Once the oil is up to temperature, cook the onion rings in small batches for 2 minutes, or until golden and crunchy. Transfer the cooked rings to kitchen paper to drain of any excess oil while you cook the remainder.

Transfer to a plate and serve hot, with your choice of sauce on the side for dipping.

Mr Singh's Fabulous Fiery Cookbook

MINTED ONIONS

KULDIP: My Granddad liked a little crunch with his daal and roti so gran would throw this quick salad together. It's really simple, but packed with flavour and transforms the simplest of dishes.

PREPARATION TIME: 5 MINUTES
COOKING TIME: N/A

Serves 4

1 large onion, thinly sliced and
    soaked in cold water for
    10 minutes
juice of ½ lemon
1 tbsp mint sauce
¼ tsp salt
1 bird's-eye chilli,
    finely chopped

Drain your sliced onions and place in a bowl. Add the rest of the ingredients and mix everything to thoroughly combine.

Serve alongside curries, daal, roti or even cold meats.

SARSON DA SAAG

This lovely dish takes time to cook but is delicious when ready. Mustard leaves can be bought from Indian supermarkets or some health-food stores, but if you can't find them, this is equally delicious when made with just spinach instead. A great vegetable side dish for any curry.

PREPARATION TIME: 1 HOUR
COOKING TIME: 2 HOURS

Serves 4

500 g/1 lb 2 oz fresh spinach leaves, coarsely chopped

300 g/10½ oz fresh mustard greens, ends trimmed and coarsely chopped

150 g/5½ oz broccoli, cut into small florets

60 g/2¼ oz fresh ginger, finely chopped

10 fresh green finger chillies, finely chopped

1 tbsp salt

50 g/1¾ oz coarse corn (maize) flour

FOR THE TARKA:

2 tbsp ghee
6 garlic cloves, crushed

Place the spinach, mustard greens, broccoli, ginger, chillies and salt into a pressure cooker with 1 litre/1¾ pints/generous 4 cups water. Stir to combine then place the pressure cooker over a low heat and seal the lid. Leave to cook for 1½ hours, then remove from the heat and set aside for another hour.

Meanwhile, make the tarka. Melt the ghee in a small frying pan or skillet over a low heat. Once melted, add the garlic and cook, stirring continuously, until golden brown, but not burned. Remove from the heat and set aside.

Carefully remove the lid from the pressure cooker then give the saag mixture a stir – the mixture should be greenish brown with a little liquid still in the base of the pan. Return the pan to the hob over a low heat and bring to a gentle simmer. Stir in the corn (maize) flour and continue to cook, stirring continuously, until thickened and creamy.

Add the tarka to the pan and stir to combine. Cook for 10 minutes more to allow the flavours of the tarka to absorb into the saag, then remove from the heat and transfer to a serving plate. Serve hot.

BREADS &
BASIC RECIPES

HANDKERCHIEF ROTI

AMAR: A lot of people are scared of making bread, but these are super simple and are ready in mintes, so are a great place for the bread novice to start. Beacuse these are so quick to make and contain only a couple of ingredients, these are our go-to breads for any midweek meal. Give them a try and you'll never buy shop-bought roti again!

PREPARATION TIME: 15 MINUTES
COOKING TIME: 10 MINUTES

Makes 4

125 g/4½ oz/1 cup plain (all-purpose) flour, plus extra for rolling

2 tbsp whole milk, at room temperature

butter, for spreading

Place the flour in a large mixing bowl and make a well in the centre. Pour the milk into the well and slowly work the flour into the liquid with your fingers. Add 4 tablespoons of water to the mixture and incorporate to form a firm dough. Set aside for 5 minutes.

Once rested, turn the dough out on to a lightly floured surface and knead for 5 minutes, until smooth. Divide the dough into 4 equal-size pieces and form each piece into a ball.

Place a chapatti pan, large frying pan or skillet over a medium heat to warm.

Dust the work surface again and then, working with one ball at a time, use a rolling pin to roll the balls into flat rounds approximately 13 cm/5 in diameter.

Place the roti on the hot pan and cook for 1 minute, then flip it over to the other side. Gently rub the top of the roti with a clean kitchen cloth and it should start to puff up. Cook for another minute, then set aside while you cook the remaining rotis.

Serve hot, brushed with butter.

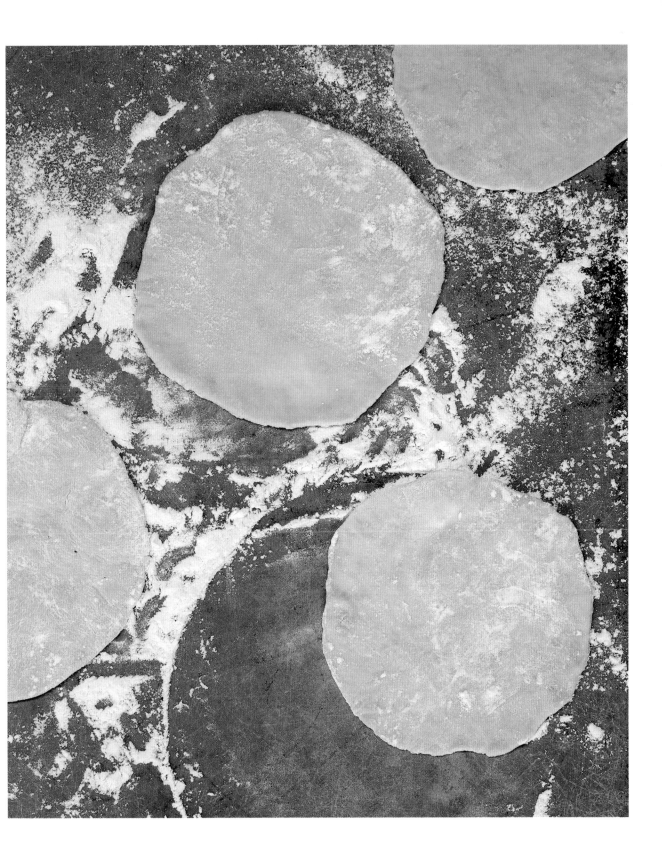

PARATHAS

MAMA SINGH: We love to eat these breads for breakfast slathered with chilli sauce and topped with egg and bacon (see page 22), but they also make a great accompaniment to any of the curries in this book. Getting the hang of folding them can take a little practise, but bear with it and you'll be a pro in no time!

PREPARATION TIME: 15 MINUTES

COOKING TIME: 10 MINUTES

Makes 4

125 g/4½ oz/1 cup plain (all-purpose) flour, plus extra for rolling

1 tsp salt

vegetable oil or melted butter, for brushing

Place the flour in a large mixing bowl and make a well in the centre. Pour the 100 ml/ 3½ fl oz/scant ½ cup lukewarm water into the well and slowly work the flour into the liquid with your fingers to form a firm dough. Set aside for 10 minutes to rest.

Place a chapatti pan, large frying pan or skillet over a medium heat to warm.

Divide the dough into 4 equal-size pieces and form each piece into a ball. Dust the work with flour then, working with one ball at a time, use a rolling pin to roll the balls into flat rounds approximately 20 cm/8 in in diameter.

Working with one paratha at a time, brush the surface with oil or butter to lightly coat. Fold the top and bottom edges of the dough circle in on themselves to create straight edges. Fold the remaining g edges in on themselves to form a square shape. Roll the paratha again to form a 20 cm/8 in square.

Brush the paratha with oil or butter on both sides again, then transfer to the hot pan and cook for 1 minute, then flip it over to the other side. Cook for another minute, then set aside while you cook the remaining paratha.

FENUGREEK FLATBREADS

KULDIP: These are a riff on the classic paratha (see opposite), but flavoured with spices and fresh fenugreek for an extra punch of flavour. They are great as a side dish or can be enjoyed as a flavoursome snack in their own right. Fresh fenugreek has a heady earthy flavour and is well worth the time in trying to source.

PREPARATION TIME: 15 MINUTES
COOKING TIME: 10 MINUTES

Makes 4

125 g/4½ oz/1 cup plain (all-purpose) flour, plus extra for rolling

1 tsp ajwain seeds

1 tsp salt

½ tsp chilli powder

½ tsp garam masala

25 g/1 oz fresh fenugreek leaves, chopped

vegetable oil or melted butter, for brushing

Place the flour in a large mixing bowl with the ajwain seeds, salt, chilli powder, garam masala and fenugreek leaves. Mix everything together and make a well in the centre with your hand. Pour the 100 ml/3½ fl oz/scant ½ cup lukewarm water into the well and slowly work the flour into the liquid with your fingers to form a firm dough. Set aside for 10 minutes to rest.

Place a chapatti pan, large frying pan or skillet over a medium heat to warm.

Divide the dough into 4 equal-size pieces and form each piece into a ball. Dust the work with flour then, working with one ball at a time, use a rolling pin to roll the balls into flat rounds approximately 20 cm/8 in in diameter.

Working with one paratha at a time, brush the surface with oil or butter to lightly coat. Fold the top and bottom edges of the dough circle in on themselves to create straight edges. Fold the remaining g edges in on themselves to form a square shape. Roll the paratha again to form a 20 cm/8 in square.

Brush the paratha with oil or butter on both sides again, then transfer to the hot pan and cook for 1 minute, then flip it over to the other side. Cook for another minute, then set aside while you cook the remaining paratha.

MAKHI DI ROTI

MAMA SINGH: These flatbreads are made with corn (maize) flour, which makes them perfect for guests who are gluten intolerent or are on low-gluten diets. These make a delicious light meal when served with Sarson da Saag (see page 137), but are equally at home with any curry.

PREPARATION TIME: 15 MINUTES
COOKING TIME: 25 MINUTES

Makes 4

125 g/4½ oz/1 cup coarse corn (maize) flour, plus extra for rolling
60 g/2¼ oz/½ cup fine corn (maize) flour
melted butter, for brushing

Place the flours in a large mixing bowl and make a well in the centre. Pour 250 ml/ 9 fl oz/generous 1 cup of hot, but not boiling water, into the well and slowly work the flour into a crumbly dough with a wooden spoon or spatula. Set aside for 5 minutes to cool.

Once cool enough to handle, turn the dough out on to a lightly floured surface and knead for 5 minutes, until smooth. Divide the dough into 4 equal-size pieces and form each piece into a ball.

Place a chapatti pan, large frying pan or skillet over a medium heat to warm.

Dust the work surface again and then, working with one ball at a time, use a rolling pin to roll the balls into flat rounds approximately 3 mm/ in thick.

Place the roti on the hot pan and cook for 3 minutes, then flip it over to the other side and cook for 5 minutes more, then set aside while you cook the remaining rotis.

Serve hot, brushed with butter.

HAND-CRUMBLED PANEER

KULDIP: The Mr Singh's office is attached to Granny Singh's home in East London. The best thing about this is that she cooks lunch for us every day. One of things that we're always asking for is this delicious hand-crumbled paneer. Cooked low and slow, whenever she makes this for us we know our taste buds are in for the time of their lives.

PREPARATION TIME: 15 MINUTES
COOKING TIME: 40 MINUTES

Serves 4

2.25 litres/4 pints/scant 9½ cups whole milk

180 ml/6 fl oz/¾ cup white vinegar

1 jar Mr Singh's Punjabi Pesto or ½ quantity Thurka (see page 152)

1 red (bell) pepper, chopped

1 green finger chilli, chopped

60 g/2¼ oz/1 cup fresh peas

1 tsp garam masala

Place the milk in large pan over a high heat. As soon as the milk starts to boil take the pan of the heat and pour in the vinegar. The milk will immediately start to separate into solid curds and watery whey, stir the mixture continuously for 2 minutes until the milk has finished separating.

Line a large sieve (strainer) with muslin and pour the mixture through it to separate the cheese curds from the liquid. Once separated, rinse the paneer under cold running water to remove any residual taste of vinegar. Bring the sides of the muslin together to enclose the paneer and squeeze to drain of any excess moisture. Set the sieve over a large bowl and set aside for 1 hour to ensure that all of the excess moisture has drained off.

Place the Punjabi Pesto or Thurka in a large pan over medium heat until bubbling, then stir in the paneer and cook, stirring occasionally for 5 minutes. Add the (bell) pepper, chilli and fresh peas and continue to cook, stirring occasionally, for 30 minutes over a low heat.

Transfer to a serving dish and sprinkle over the garam masala. Serve cooled.

HOT CHILLI SAUCE

POPS: This isn't our classic chilli sauce (as that recipe is a well-guarded secret), but is a good alternative and something that I often knock up for a family barbecue at home. Though it packs some serious heat, the key to a great chilli sauce is a balance, so here mango and mint provide some depth of flavour and relief from the spice.

PREPARATION TIME: 15 MINUTES
COOKING TIME: 10 MINUTES

Makes 2 small bottles

2 large bunches mint, leaves
    picked
4 large green mangos
40 g/1½ oz green bird's-eye
    chillies, chopped
1 tbsp salt
1½ tbsp honey
juice of ½ lime

Place the mint leaves in a small pan and pour over water to cover. Place the pan over a medium heat and bring to boil. Cook for 3 minutes, then strain the mint leaves and transfer to a blender. Blend the leaves to a fine paste, then place in a sieve (strainer) set over a bowl. Using a wooden spoon or spatula, push the mint paste through the sieve into the bowl to create a fine puree. Set aside.

Peel the mangos, remove the central seed and roughly chop the flesh. Place the mango flesh in a small pan and add water to cover. Place the pan over a medium heat and bring to the boil. Cook for 3 minutes, then strain the mango and transfer the cooked flesh to a blender. Blend the mango to a fine paste, then place in a sieve (strainer) set over a bowl. Using a wooden spoon or spatula, push the mango paste through the sieve into the bowl to create a fine puree. Set aside.

Return the mango and mint pastes back to the blender and add the rest of the ingredients. Blend the mixture to a smooth sauce. If the mixture is too liquid, cook it gently over a medium heat until thickened.

Leave the sauce to cool, then transfer to sterilised bottles. This will keep for up to 2 weeks in a refrigerator.

Mr Singh's Fabulous Fiery Cookbook

SWEET CHILLI SAUCE

POPS: Odd as it sounds, I find some sweet chilli sauces too sweet. This recipe relies on the natural sweetness of cherries and doesn't have and added sugar, which adds a delicious background sweetness that doesn't overpower the sauce. Though this is technically a 'sweet' sauce, it still packs a punch.

PREPARATION TIME: 15 MINUTES
COOKING TIME: 10 MINUTES

Makes 2 small bottles

140 g/5 oz fresh cherries

30 g/1 oz scotch bonnet
   chillies, chopped

30 g/1 oz red bird's-eye chillies,
   chopped

1 tbsp salt

3 tbsp honey

juice of 1 lemon

Place the cherries in a small pan and pour over water to cover. Place the pan over a medium heat and bring to boil. Cook for 3 minutes, then strain the cherries and transfer to a blender. Blend the leaves to a fine paste, then place in a sieve (strainer) set over a bowl. Using a wooden spoon or spatula, push the cherry paste through the sieve into the bowl to create a fine puree. Set aside.

Return the cherry puree back to the blender and add the rest of the ingredients. Blend the mixture to a smooth sauce. If the mixture is too liquid, cook it gently over a medium heat until thickened.

Cool the sauce and bottle. This will keep for 2 weeks in a refrigerator.

THURKA

POPS: This sauce is the base recipe for many Punjabi meals, so you can make a big batch and freeze it if you're going to be cooking from this book a lot (and why wouldn't you be?!). At Mr Singh's, we bottle this and sell it as 'Punjabi Pesto' as it is every bit as versatile as the classic Italian staple.

PREPARATION TIME: 5 MINUTES
COOKING TIME: 40 MINUTES

Serves 4

3 tbsp vegetable or
   sunflower oil

2 onions, coarsely grated

4 garlic cloves, crushed

1 x 400 g/14 oz tin chopped
   tomatoes, blended until
   smooth

thumb-size piece fresh ginger,
   grated

2 green finger chillies,
   finely chopped

1 tsp cumin seeds

1½ tsp salt

1 tsp ground turmeric

Place the oil in a large pan over medium heat. Once hot, add the onion and garlic and cook, stirring continuously, until golden, around 20 minutes.

Add the tomatoes to the pan and continue to cook, stirring occasionally, for another 10 minutes. Add the ginger, cumin, salt and turmeric to the pan and continue to cook for 10 minutes more. The sauce is ready when the oil starts to pool on the surface. Use the sauce immediately or cool and refrigerate/freeze for later use.

CONTENTS OF THE PUNJABI MASALA TIN

Listed below are the most commonly used spices in Punjabi cooking. Indian supermarkets are a great place to buy your spices as they are often sold more cheaply and in larger quantities than supermarkets. Do clear out your spice cupboard every six months or so as spices lose their potency quickly and the flavour of your food will suffer because of it.

Chilli Powder (Lall Mirch)

Chilli Powder is available in two strengths, it can be hot or extra hot as per your preference. You may need to experiment to get the heat that you prefer but a level teaspoon per recipe is generally enough.

Cumin Seeds (Jeera)

These pungent brownish seeds look similar to caraway. They impart and deep, earthy flavour to dishes and are deliciously pungent when dry roasted and ground. Just as delicious sprinkled over simple yogurt and salads as in complex curries.

Black Mustard Seeds (Rai)

These tiny black purplish-brown seeds have a powerful bitter taste and a small quantity goes a long way. To get the most from them, they are cooked in hot oil until they pop and release their lovely pungent flavour.

Fenugreek Seeds (Methi)

These are tiny mustard coloured seeds with a very bitter taste. They can be used whole or crushed, but must be sizzled in hot oil before incorporating into dishes to relese their complex flavour.

Turmeric (Haldi)

This distinctively hued powder is revered for its rich yellow colour and healing powers. It has an earthy taste with a slight metallic tang and is used in small quantities when cooking. Its rich colour can easily stain your hands and clothes, so use with care.

Garam Masala

Every Punjabi home will have a different recipe for garam masala, though you can also buy it ready made. It is a spice mix that contains 10 different herbs and herbs that are roasted and ground to a fine powder. It is generally added to curries at the end of the cooking process to add a lovely vibrant aroma.

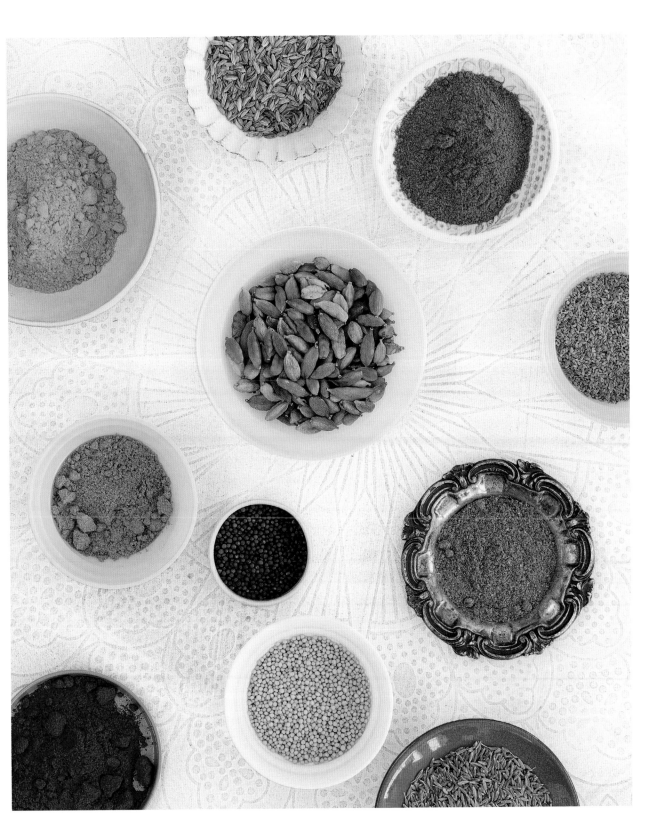

INDEX

Mr Singh's Fabulous Fiery Cookbook

ACKNOWLEDGEMENTS

To you, the reader: it means so much that you have chosen
this book. We hope our story and recipes give your family and
friends years of happy, tasty memories. And to those of you who
championed or purchased Mr. Singh's: you have our eternal love
and gratitude.

To our close family and friends: we thank you so much for
all that you have done to help get us to where we are today.
We are grateful for every kind word and helpful deed.

Special thanks to Bham, Pit, Vikas, Zorba, Investors, Jinder Mamaji
and Nana Chacha. Thank you for the graft and for the belief.

Polly, Emily and the rest of the Pavilion team – thank you for
believing in us and for wanting to share our journey with the
world. You are beyond awesome!

The Publisher's would also like to extend their thanks to project
editor Daniel Hurst, designer Laura Russell, photographer John
Carey, Katie Marshall and Eliza Baird for home economy and Lucy
Harvey for prop styling.